Improv for LAWYERS

A Lawyer's Guide To Ignoring The Inner Critic, Listening Empathetically and Telling Winning Stories At Trial

Honorable Terence F. MacCarthy

Improv for LAWYERS

A Lawyer's Guide To
Ignoring The Inner Critic,
Listening Empathetically and
Telling Winning Stories At Trial

Published by
Glissando Strings Publishing, LLC
glissandostrings@yahoo.com

Printed in the United States of America

Book cover design by Annie Donlin
Interior layout design by Vickie Swisher, Studio 20/20

ISBN 978-0-578-45956-1 (softcover)

DEDICATION

To two champions of justice to whom I am indebted for their love, support and mentorship.

To Donald Fiedler, an innovative Trial Advocacy teacher with whom I had the privilege and pleasure of successfully training lawyers with Improv. While driving together across Ireland many years ago, I told Don this book would become a reality.

To my father, Terence MacCarthy, for dedicating countless hours teaching and inspiring lawyers for more than fifty five years with groundbreaking Trial Advocacy.

SPECIAL THANKS TO THE FOLLOWING FOR SHARING THEIR SIGNIFICANT TALENTS

Phoenix Tyler (C. Phoenix Tyler Productions), Robert Walker (Exam Zone), Anna Shilov Sterk (Law Office of Anna Shilov Sterk), Annie Donlin (Redfish Design) and Jack Parker Ward. And of course I am indebted to the inspiration of Jude, Catherine, Terence and Patrick.

Improv for LAWYERS

A Lawyer's Guide To Ignoring The Inner Critic, Listening Empathetically and Telling Winning Stories At Trial

FOREWORD

Judge Terry MacCarthy, then a public defender in Chicago, taught my Opening Statement Seminar at the National Criminal Defense College in 2000. Lively, full of humor, and encouraging, MacCarthy coaxed our group of new public defenders towards maximum openness and creativity in developing our presentations. We were practicing the extremely powerful techniques of improv! MacCarthy has been teaching these techniques for 20 plus years, informed by his more than 500 trials as an attorney and a true love for the practice of improvisation.

I saw two great performances that year, and I can still remember the faces of both actors. The first was James Gammon (outshining Nolte, Penn, and Harrelson) in Sam Shepherd's San Francisco production of *The Late Henry Moss*. The second was an opening statement in MacCarthy's class. These were brilliant performances, and one was by a novice public defender, whom MacCarthy had coached over a few days. Both performances were memorable because of the feelings displayed by the performers, but that was only a product of something more important: the abandonment to the role, ego-be-damned. MacCarthy had asked his student to consider his opening statement with the greatest level of creativity and openness, to try something very different, to accept what the case had given him and let go. The student told the story of a tragic accident from the perspective of a powerless and horrified nursery room wall. I have since spent hundreds of hours in federal court as a public defender, and I have not seen many courtroom performances that were better.

Improv is a powerful tool in court and on stage. Since 2000, I have written and performed on stage with the comedy group Kasper Hauser, which I co-founded with the three other current members. Kasper Hauser has written five books, including *Sky Maul* and the best seller *Obama's Blackberry*. We have appeared on *This American Life, All Things Considered,* and *Marketplace* and written for BBC TV, and HBO Digital Productions. We have written and performed with many of the world's funniest people and played great venues like Edinburgh's Gilded Balloon, the Palace of Fine Arts, and the Geary Theater. Kasper Hauser is not an improv troupe. We write and edit obsessively and collaboratively, fighting over every word. But Kasper Hauser relies on improv techniques to generate much of our content. Improvisation is an infinite resource.

I once called Terry MacCarthy to brainstorm an opening statement I was preparing to give in federal court. His answer to me was a complete surprise, because it was based on improv techniques. And it worked; it led to a successful outcome at trial. I am grateful to MacCarthy for putting a lifetime of high-level trial work and cutting edge advocacy training into a form that a reader can take home and begin practicing immediately, without attending an elite Trial Advocacy program.

Courtroom lawyers hoping to substantially improve their art and improvisers and actors who teach and train lawyers need to read this book. It is the best manual bridging improv and trial law, and, if you practice the techniques, it will be the beginning of a journey full of surprises, which are, after all, the building blocks of creativity and courtroom success.

John Reichmuth
Nov. 15, 2017

I.

INTRODUCTION

"Every child is an artist. The problem is how to remain an artist once we grow up."

— Pablo Picasso

For trial lawyers and trial advocacy teachers, even those with a modicum of experience in comedy or acting, the thought of doing improv is intimidating. Add the assumption, albeit false, that one has to be exceptionally funny to do improv, and the idea is daunting.

Reluctantly and apprehensively putting all doubts aside, I dipped my toes into improv waters many years ago to have some fun, a few laughs, and really, to see what it was all about. To say the least, it was interesting, fun and challenging, and of course, we had many laughs along the way.

Admittedly, my interest then was not improv for the sake of improv, but rather, how to use improv exercises to train trial lawyers. It was immediately apparent that improv incorporated effectively into trial advocacy training. Through improv lawyers become more effective and powerful advocates, persuaders and storytellers.

Many lawyers share a lack of meaningful experience with acting or comedy. Anticipating and eventually confirming their reluctance and apprehension about improv, I did two things before using improv in training plans. I often changed the name and I compartmentalized the exercises.

First, recognizing that "everything is in a name," I often refer to the improv exercises as "communication exercises." Remembering a young niece with a finicky appetite who would not eat much outside of hot dogs and French fries, I recalled a waiter bringing lamb sweetbreads (the throat glands of the lamb) to the table. When my niece inquired about the dish, I said they were "tenders," and she ate the whole plate of "tenders," enjoying every morsel. Clearly, everything was "in a name." Likewise, the phrase "communication exercises," sounds harmless, unintimidating, and after all, what lawyer does not want to be a better communicator?

Second, I compartmentalize the improv exercises somewhat, because although many improv exercises develop different skills simultaneously, lawyers more immediately grasp and accept *what* we do when they understand *how* the exercises benefit courtroom performance.

As with any training technique for trial lawyers or otherwise, the proof was in the pudding. After utilizing improv at numerous trial advocacy seminars and classes, the improv exercises received unanimously positive feedback. Lawyers note that improv is actually *fun*, and although it takes them out of their comfort zone, they greatly enjoy the experience and actually want to do more. While some trial training programs are arduous, and at times, dare I say boring, improv training inevitably keeps lawyers involved, interested, and longing for more, because they view it as fun, not work. Incidentally, lawyers learn through the process there is no pressure to be funny or quick witted as anticipated, but rather that the many laughs result simply and naturally from the *collaborative* group effort, and often from making other people look good.

Lawyers also prefer exposure to improv early on in a trial advocacy program because the exercises help knock their inner critic, or inner censor, off their shoulder. Most lawyers, and in fact most public speakers, acknowledge an imaginary little person standing on their shoulder, critiquing and often second guessing and doubting their performance. While trying to perform at the optimum level and focus on the task at hand, the inner critic runs interference. Improv effectively helps eradicate self-doubt and increase self-confidence by teaching lawyers to ignore the inner critic. After completing this process, lawyers inevitably perform better during a training program, and of course, in the courtroom.

Lawyers note many other byproducts of improv that effectively build the skills necessary to becoming more powerful persuaders and storytellers, including emotional range, developing different points of view, paying attention and developing real listening skills. Unlike many lawyers, whose idea of listening is talking and waiting to talk, they learn to listen empathetically and stay in tune with their surroundings.

Improv not only develops the ability to listen effectively, but also to prepare and present a courtroom story taking into account the *jury's* perspective. We best learn and understand most communication skills from the standpoint of our audience. Improv instills the ability to look beyond ourselves and understand that our courtroom story inevitably ends up in the most important place, the jury deliberation room.

With emphasis on being in the moment, lawyers gain the ability to "think on their feet." Extemporaneous speaking is frightening, but something we all did without fear until the age of three or four. Then, perhaps after immersion into academia and the unrelenting, guiding principle of "right and wrong," we lost that ability. Through improv, lawyers reclaim the gift of spontaneity that serves them well in court.

Admittedly, some people "think on their feet" better and quicker than others. But like anything else, through practice, exercise and the development of muscles in our brain, we improve our ability to "think on our feet," which is perhaps merely a fancier phrase for reacting. We always, and rightfully so, emphasize thorough trial preparation, yet experience allows that things do not always go as planned.

When those unplanned moments hit, the ability to react effectively serves a lawyer well and improv trains lawyers to react and present cases with unconscious capability.

Reincorporation, another improv skill, morphs into trial advocacy as the classic rhetorical device, repetition. Used at times by trial lawyers when "looping," this skill helps jurors' retention and memory. Additionally, as lawyers "loop" during voir dire, they connect with jurors by acknowledging the lawyer's digestion of a potential juror's answer.

Improv relies on collaboration and team building, skills that serve us well in court in both obvious and not so obvious ways, such as dealing with adversarial witnesses. And last but not least, improv embeds in lawyers the important and effective "Yes and...," mentality.

THE TRIAL LAWYER: PERSUADER AND STORYTELLER

A good trial lawyer's skills are vast and varied. Lawyers and perhaps people in general, given popular culture's obsession with courtroom drama, try to put their finger on what creates the essence of a good trial lawyer and effective trial presentations. In truth, several components, or skills, make trial lawyers effective. The interplay among these skills makes lawyers successful, enabling them to function at an optimum level in the courtroom.

Good trial lawyers are effective *communicators* who use language, body language, and expression, to name just a few skills, in the courtroom. Through their unique interpretation and delivery of a set of facts, they *persuade* jurors to side with them.

Undoubtedly, trial advocacy has evolved such that most who teach trial advocacy acknowledge that a good trial lawyer is indeed a good persuader, but also an effective *storyteller*. Every case has unique facts, strengths and weaknesses. After incorporating these facts as well as the emotions and appropriate law into a case theory, the case evolves into the form of a story. All other things being equal, the lawyer who captures and convinces the jurors with the most creatively crafted and powerfully told story will prevail. After all, legalese is nonsense. A good story is user friendly.

THE "PRACTICE" OF LAW

Though real clients with liberty or money at stake may be dismayed by the idea, lawyers do actually "practice" law. That is to say, lawyers continually learn and improve while "practicing" law in the courtroom. The essential skills necessary for trying cases are to some extent, and necessarily given the nature of the job, honed on the job during trials. Lawyers constantly learn from both successes and failures in the courtroom, and many of the lessons learned contribute to future courtroom successes. Thus, while the courtroom is a place for "performance" where a trial lawyer puts forth the finished product of a case, it is also a place of great learning, where, as experience tells us, we hone our skills.

THE ZONE

The unique experience of trying a case often involves pressure-packed situations demanding that lawyers make hundreds of split-second decisions that have significant ramifications. Many of these split-second decisions can and will often be the difference between winning and losing. Certainly, the aggregate of these decisions undoubtedly weighs on the minds of jurors and impacts their verdict.

Given the unique nature of trying a case, most trial lawyers operate at a different level, or on a different plane, in the courtroom. Most are in a zone, focused solely on the task at hand, and oblivious to anything collateral to the trial, even eating or sleeping. While in this unique zone, trial lawyers by necessity and at times, perhaps unconsciously, use certain muscles of the brain that are otherwise unnecessary and probably not accessed in their daily lives.

Skills associated with trying cases are to some extent honed while in that zone during trials. Undoubtedly, however, those same skills can and must be honed to every extent possible before stepping in a courtroom. A trial lawyer must develop skills to effectively prepare and present their case, but also, they must prepare for the rigors of a trial, to function most effectively in court on their feet when in that zone.

How can a lawyer best refine the skills of case preparation and persuasive presentation? How can a lawyer develop and prepare the brain muscles one uses in court? How can a lawyer best simulate the courtroom experience of being put "on the spot"? What is the best way to learn how to try a case?

TRIAL ADVOCACY TRAINING

Trial advocacy training, like most other art forms, has undergone great transformations. There was a time when lawyers learned only the "pillage and plunder" method. The method was adversarial to a fault and cross examination, in particular, was used most often to engage opposing witnesses in unnecessary, bloody confrontations. Many advocates bullied witnesses while jurors frequently sided with the witnesses, spilling only the lawyer's blood onto the courtroom floor.

Trial lawyers eventually turned to acting and psycho-drama to enhance their craft. Training in both areas certainly helped lawyers improve their communication skills, and psycho-drama in particular, helped them learn to spontaneously dramatize different scenes and roles, particularly in brainstorming cases.

Recognizing the persuasive power of stories, lawyers also worked with storytelling. We cannot deny the power of a good story. Since prehistoric times people have narrated stories to communicate history, to educate and to entertain. From cave drawings to Dr. Suess, stories have effectively related facts in a magical way that intimately touches both the heart and mind, while creating a clear memory in the listener's mind.

Like storytelling, improv dates back to the beginning of man, as we know that long before written language, people acted out stories. This book uses improv to enhance trial skills and provide lawyers with the skills necessary to try cases. Through improv exercises, trial lawyers develop an arsenal that encompasses and exceeds the benefits of most other methods of trial advocacy training.

IMPROV FOR THE TRIAL LAWYER

This book is not about improv for the sake of improv. Indeed, improv books are worthy of individual books in their own right and have been written. Rather, this book tailors and discusses improv to demonstrate how improv benefits trial lawyers by teaching practical and effective courtroom skills, not the least of which is how to effectively craft and most persuasively tell a client's story at trial, from both a theoretical and practical standpoint. We discuss some topics that are not unique to improv because they cover basic and effective communication skills.

For purposes of this book, the term "story" refers only to the "story" of a client, in no way suggesting the telling of a lie, falsehood or fiction. It in no way suggests we should put forth fictionalized, false or perjured testimonial evidence in court. Likewise, the term "character" refers to any person, often times a witness, that played a role in the story we tell in court, just as we refer to a character in a play, story, or movie.

Incidentally, some lawyers assume we only tell stories during opening statement and closing argument, as these two areas are usually associated with storytelling. However, there is a significant storytelling component to every part of a trial, including, but not limited to voir dire, cross-examination and direct examination. On some level, we tell our client's story, and at times stories by analogy, during each and every part of the trial.

Improv is generally done in a group setting, focusing largely on collaboration and team-building. Unfortunately, because of the time constraints and hectic schedules inherent in practicing law, it simply is not always practical for many lawyers to regularly attend improv classes or seminars. This book cannot, nor does it intend to replace those experiences, as admittedly, many communication skills are gained "by doing." However, it benefits lawyers and Trial Advocacy teachers by demonstrating techniques and exercises, used in either a group setting or alone, that translate into effective and improved trial skills, given a willingness to adopt and apply the techniques. Many of these principles apply as well to negotiations and appellate work.

There is often sentiment among experienced lawyers that they have learned the ropes and therefore cannot and do not need to develop and improve as lawyers and communicators. But like medicine, law truly is a "practice," and undoubtedly all lawyers can improve as persuaders. Some lawyers, stuck in their ways, simply don't want to take time to get better. Most of the best trial lawyers, however, always strive to get better. Based on the premise that every trial lawyer can get better at their trade, this book offers new insight for both new and experienced lawyers seeking to elevate their courtroom skills.

This book further serves as a guide for Trial Advocacy teachers and professional actors who train both inexperienced and experienced lawyers alike, as it develops new skills and enhances and improves existing skills. Admittedly, some of the exercises will be a bit unusual and feel silly. Even the silly games however, help develop critical courtroom skills. To be certain, while improv is more about collaboration than comedy, many of the exercises will be funny and evoke plenty of laughter.

THE FOUR NECESSARY (AND ONLY) RULES OF IMPROV FOR TRAINING LAWYERS

Though the exact number varies, improv artists extoll, live and abide by several rules, often as many as ten or more. The good news for training lawyers is we only need four rules, and when we follow these four rules, an improv based training will succeed and be fruitful.

YES AND/ACCEPT THE OFFER

The first, and perhaps most significant rule, is to "accept the offer," by abiding by the "Yes and..." rule. Incidentally, while this rule is critical to improv and effective in the courtroom, it is also successful in dealing with business and relationships. Let's talk about its importance to improv, and life generally, and then talk about the rule's specific value to lawyers.

The "yes and..." rule involves accepting the premise one has been given by responding with a "yes and" mind set and building on that premise. Let's use a fictitious skit for example. Janet says to Steve, "Hey Steve, do you know where my football jersey is?" If not "accepting the offer," Steve says, "You don't have a football jersey, you've never watched a game of football in your life and I don't know what you are talking about." In improv this is called blocking, as the person playing Steve did not accept the offer, but rather, closed the door on the potential development of the story's original premise.

To accept the offer in the skit, Steve replies to the same question with something like the following: "Yes, Janet, you left your Bears jersey on the washing machine on Sunday like you do after every Bears win, and like a good husband, I washed it." In this second response, Steve accepts the offer. He builds on the original premise, encouraging the skit to continue and the story to grow. Incidentally, we now know some of the who, what, when and where of the skit: Janet and Steve are a married couple who regularly watch the Bears.

Using another example from a fictitious skit, person one says, "Hey Pete, you've always been a great neighbor – do you mind if I use your snow blower?" In not accepting the offer, person two says, "I don't go by Pete, I don't live close to you and there is no snow in the forecast." Again, person two has rejected the offer, and closed the door on the initial idea, effectively ending the story. To accept the offer, person two says, "Of course, you can use my snow blower, Bob! We've been neighbors for 20 years and that's the least I can do as the godfather to your child."

When blocking, or not accepting an offer, the flow of ideas stops, effectively halting progress and destroying ideas. In both improv and real life, the "yes and..." rule encourages and develops positive, fruitful communication. The listener *acknowledges and builds upon* an idea and thus, further develops and creates ideas based on the previous premise. The "yes and" mindset creates cooperation and innovation, thereby encouraging more openness and less ego.

While on trial, and notably during voir dire, the skill of acknowledging and validating ideas is invaluable. Among other things, it creates trust. Unfortunately, the dominant conversational theme of many law students and lawyers is to respond with "Yes, but...,." or some variation thereof.

By reputation and in reality, a lawyer's natural inclination to argue with everyone about almost anything is often to their own detriment. We have all met and likely been put off by legally educated, formerly open minded people. We later discuss the negative impact of this attitude in court, and why succumbing to the temptation to constantly argue with people is distasteful to jurors.

Using our "yes and..." mentality, we reverse the approach learned in law school, as we learn to accept the offer given and roll with it. Incidentally, the "yes and...," approach also works effectively with mediations, negotiations and appellate advocacy.

PAY ATTENTION AND LISTEN

Our second rule is to listen and pay attention. Effective listening is a critical courtroom skill and we should teach speaking skills in conjunction with listening skills. It sounds easy enough. Yet lawyers as a group are not always known for *empathetic* listening, particularly in court. They often miss out on significant and critical comments of witnesses and opposing counsel, while spectators and at times co-counsels pick up on these things. Why, for that matter, can some lawyers remember potential jurors' names during voir dire, while others find this next to impossible? Perhaps we can point to nerves or being wrapped up in their "script" and what to say next.

Regardless, many lawyers simply do not listen empathetically to their surroundings. Too often they view listening as talking and waiting to talk. Interestingly, while all trial advocacy courses emphasize and focus on speaking skills, too few ever work on developing effective listening skills. The ability to focus on the here and now by listening empathetically drastically improves a lawyer's courtroom performance. All trial advocacy courses, to some extent, should have a significant listening component. Similar to speaking skills, effective listening skills can develop and improve.

Most trial lawyers have walked back to counsel table before completing a cross examination to see if their trial partner has "anything further," only to have their partner say something like, "Didn't you hear the witness say the car was green?" Assuming the green car was important to the case, the cross examiner did not hear it most likely because they did not listen empathetically. They were simply talking and waiting to talk.

Actors do not simply wait for their next line to know when to speak. They immerse themselves in the whole scene and the entire conversation. Through improv we focus on being in the moment and listening empathetically. This skill allows lawyers to focus, digest and react ("think on your feet," as it is commonly known) persuasively in court.

INVEST WITHOUT WORRYING ABOUT MISTAKES

The third rule is that one must *invest* in the task and willingly experiment without worry about making mistakes. In the words of Miles Davis, "Do not fear mistakes, there are none." Similarly, Grover Porter says, "It is more important to be human than to be perfect." Most lawyers, and in fact most public speakers, often have an inner critic on their shoulder as they speak. This imaginary critic whispers to them and interrupts with critical analysis *while* they perform.

Learning to invest without worry is a first step toward developing the ability to ignore the inner critic. *After* completing a performance, we might consult our little imaginary friend, but doing so during a performance is counterproductive. Indeed, we focus on *what* we're doing, not *how* we're doing, and to function in court at the highest level, we need to flick that little person off our shoulder.

Before going to school, toddlers are fearlessly creative storytellers. They venture without hesitation into the land of make believe and extemporaneous speaking. With no constant, lingering inner censor telling them what is "right" and "wrong," they improvise fearlessly. This fearlessness often ends after exposure to an academic system where "right" and "wrong" becomes the standard and grades, "achievement" and success depend largely, if not entirely, on the ability to give "right" answers.

If you ask a toddler to say "once upon a time...," and tell you a story, they typically and without hesitation roll into an extemporaneous, improvised story, without worry of failure or right or wrong. Ask the same question of an adult, or even a child who has been committed to and experienced our academic system, and a likely response is, "About what?" They have difficulty getting the story off the ground largely because of stifled creativity due to a developed inner critic and fear of being "wrong." Similarly, when asking a toddler to simply "say a word," they generally immediately spout off a word. However, the same demand of an adult likely produces the response, "about what?"

Through improv we *relearn* to function and speak extemporaneously and without worry about our self-limiting inner critic. We develop and improve our ability to think on our feet in court.

Perhaps the phrase, "think on your feet," actually makes the skill sound like a magical, one person in a hundred skill. Admittedly, some people do "think on their feet" more effectively than others. But many of them, comedians and actors in particular, developed and improved this skill by practicing improv. Regardless, it is not magic, but rather, simply the ability to *react* effectively.

Now we note a disclaimer. There are of course, "right" and "wrong" things to say in court. For the most part trials are not improvised or extemporaneous, but rather well thought out, thoroughly prepared presentations. Indeed, thorough preparation is the axis around which the whole trial process spins. Well prepared lawyers win more often than not, and at times, they win solely on the basis of their thorough preparation. Yet typically, no trial goes entirely as planned, and lawyers constantly make extemporaneous decisions that affect the case outcome. Hence, we need to develop and improve our ability to react.

DON'T BE SCATOLOGICAL

The fourth and final rule: Don't be scatological. As we saw above, when people block and refuse to accept an offer, they extinguish an idea. Likewise, succumbing to the constant temptation in improv to turn scatological, usually for an easy and cheap laugh, will with few exceptions cause creative ideas to fizzle out. Sex lines are one example.

Inevitably, when a skit turns scatological, the story hits a dead end and fizzles out.

In this regard children are really no different than adults. When children play and their discussion turns to "poopy" or "farting," the discussion becomes landlocked by that idea and never escapes that turn. Adults are no different, as an idea or skit that turns to sex, illness or death, tends to similarly become landlocked by preventing any meaningful development. Stories, in particular, find nowhere to go, as inevitably the scatological leads the story to a slow, painful death.

II.

IMPROV WARM UP: LEARNING TO FOCUS, LISTEN AND IGNORE THE INNER CRITIC

"If you hear a voice within you say, 'you can not paint,' then by all means paint, and that voice will be silenced."

— Vincent Van Gogh

"Do not fear mistakes. There are none."

— Miles Davis

"Nothing will stop you from being creative so effectively as the fear of making a mistake."

— John Cleese

"When you talk you are only repeating what you already know. But if you listen, you may learn something new."

— Dalai Lama

Through a series of exercises we warm up much like an athlete warms up before a sporting event. We loosen up while simultaneously learning to pay attention, focus and begin the process of becoming empathetic listeners. Also, although not necessarily consciously known to participants, we develop collaboration, spontaneity and other skills. While suggesting several exercises that have all proven helpful in training lawyers, there is no limit as to how many or which exercises will achieve our goals. We can add many additional exercises. We can make them up or tweak versions of the exercises discussed. These exercises are fun and productive and few people consider them as actual "work."

To loosen up and start focusing and listening, the group stands in a circle. With a simple game like "Zip Zap Zop," the group will necessarily start focusing. To start the game, one person exclaims "zip!" while simultaneously clapping their hands and "sending" the signal toward another person in the group while making eye contact with that person. The recipient then performs the same clap and eye contact to anyone else in the group, this time saying "zap!" The next person receiving the prompt will repeat the process, this time saying "zop!" The game proceeds randomly with the players eventually pushed to play at increasing speeds. Once comfortable with the format, we play as fast as humanly possible, and to add a mildly competitive element to the game, any player that makes a mistake gracefully exits the group until only two or three people remain.

A similar game, perhaps a bit sillier and also eliciting laughs, is "Bunny Bunny." While standing in a circle, three people, one in the center and the people immediately to the left and right of the center person, continuously exclaim "Bunny, bunny, bunny, bunny, bunny ...." The middle person moves both sets of their index and ring fingers up and down in front of their mouth to simulate the bunny's large teeth. The person to the left of the center person holds their right hand down at their side and their left hand up in the air at their side to simulate the left bunny ear. The person on the right does the opposite, with left hand down at their side and right hand up to simulate the right bunny ear. All three continuously chant "bunny, bunny, bunny...," until the center person deliberately and with eye contact "sends" the bunny signal to another, random player, with a louder than usual "Bunny!" command. The new recipient then becomes the teeth and the people to their right and left become the respective ears, with the three new people proceeding similarly to the first group. The group carries on and any player making a mistake exits the group until only three or four people remain.

Both "zip zap zop" and "bunny bunny" demand great focus and the whole group must pay attention. On another level, they learn to make mistakes without feeling repercussion or embarrassment. They act silly and react without thinking, which is a great first step toward thinking on their feet and ignoring their inner critic.

Taking the warm up to a different level, we tell "one word" stories. Also played in the circle, the group tells a story with each person adding only one word to the story. The sequence is not random. Rather, the group proceeds around the circle in succession. Players must not succumb to the temptation to say more than one word.

After trying the exercise slowly, the group focuses on two things. First, they move the story around the circle as quickly as possible. This prevents the players from *thinking*. As they add their word to the story, they simply *react*. The temptation to think about what they might say while the story is several players away disappears, as they realize they cannot possibly know what to say until the person immediately before them speaks.

Second, as the story moves around the circle quickly, the group aims to tell a story with a beginning, middle and end. They collectively recite a narrative resembling an actual story, rather than nonsensical rant.

To add one more exercise, perhaps we do the following: "One hundred eighty five ________ walk into a bar and the bartender says, 'We don't serve ________ here.' And the ________ says ....'" The three blanks are filled in with the same word, and the person reciting the sentence improvises the last sentence with a statement that plays off that word. For instance, the operative word is "tennis ball." Each person recites the full statement, inserting the word "tennis ball" into the blanks. The last line might be, "are you going to bounce me out of here," or, "what kind of racquet is this anyway?"

Through just a few of the unlimited number of warm ups, we encourage and develop empathetic listening, collaboration (and confidence in one another) and keen focus. We develop effective reaction skills and nudge our inner critic off our shoulder.

To fully develop and commit to the concept of accepting the offer, we practice starting scenes. During this exercise, the group forms two straight lines in front of one another, with each person paired up with someone from the other side. On a command to start, each person on one side of the line starts an improvised skit with a line or two of dialogue involving fictitious characters. The person across from them accepts the offer and responds in a way that develops the skit.

After two or three lines from each person, or about twenty seconds, the partners' goal is to reveal the who, what, when and where of the relationship to an audience (or usually a pretend audience). After about twenty seconds, the group is instructed to stop that skit, perhaps with a clap of the hands, and each person slides down the line, in "round robin" fashion, lining up in front of a new partner. After about two to three seconds, or only as long as it takes the group to slide down to a new partner, a clap instructs the group to start a new and different skit. Each new skit uses different characters, places and relationships, and this process repeats many times.

For instance, person one, while holding their right knee, says, "Doctor Smith, thanks for the office visit! The steroid shot worked wonders and I think I can play in Friday night's game." Person two, accepting the offer, says, "Well, Susan, I've been treating you for seven years and typically you've never had problems playing after the shot, except for the time you stopped the puck with your knee to win the state championship three years ago." Person one then says, "Doctor Smith, who would have ever guessed that my father's college roommate would have gotten my knee in shape so I could play on an Olympic team!" Each person then adds perhaps one or two more lines of dialogue, and after about 20 seconds, the skit stops, and the exercise proceeds as described above, with a fresh skit created each time.

This example demonstrates the purpose of the skit. Within two lines of dialogue we understand a significant amount about the who, what, when and where of the relationship. We accomplish this by adhering to the "yes and..." rule. Our doctor - patient relationship, occurring in the office, is long term, and Dr. Smith was a college roommate of Susan's father. Susan is, of course, an accomplished hockey player.

The "yes and" rule is imperative for this exercise to work, and the process of creating (and letting go of) many new skits in rapid fire succession ensures that everyone is well equipped to "think on their feet." Incidentally, most lawyers have witnessed an ineffective opening statement where several minutes into the presentation, the jury has little to no understanding about the case. By the time the jury has sufficient context for the story, most of what was said previously is lost upon them. This exercise emphasizes the need to allow a jury to immediately grasp relationships and story context.

To continue warming up, this time by creating narratives, we follow up the "one word" stories by using a prompt to create a story backbone. This exercise creates trust among the group and develops the ability to spontaneously and collaboratively create narratives, while further refining listening and reacting skills. We use a storytelling format we discuss in more detail later as a means of accessing the backbone to a case story.

While standing in a circle, a group improvises a story by adding more than one word, perhaps two or three sentences each, to the following prompts:

"Once upon a time...
Every day...
But one day...
Because of that...
Because of that...
Because of that...
Until finally...
The moral of the story is...."

Proceeding in order around the circle, each person shares part of a cohesive story. For example, player one recites "Once upon a time," and adds two or three sentences of a story, followed by player two, who says, "Every day...," and adds another part of the story, and so on. Similar to the one word story, players tell the spontaneous story without "thinking" about what to say. They merely listen to previous offerings and quickly react effectively and spontaneously, adding to the story without concern of "right" or "wrong." Due to the prompts, the group will naturally tell a complete story, with a beginning, middle and end.

After a solid and mixed set of warm up exercises, several good things happen. The group accepts the four rules and recognizes the value of those rules. They no longer fear mistakes because they learn to ignore their inner critic and loosen up the brain muscles that enable them to react quickly and effectively. For purposes of training, they willingly invest in their own development while trusting in and collaborating with the group. These are some of the baby steps toward becoming a more powerful persuader in court.

There are two more steps, however, before continuing. The first is to get the group better in tune with one another. To do so, the group stands in a circle with their eyes closed and each person *randomly* counts out loud, trying to count as high as possible, without anyone speaking over someone else. When, and it will happen, especially initially, any two people speak at the same time, the count resumes at "one." This exercise repeats until the group reaches a significantly high number by demonstrating comfort with silence and a willingness to speak in "turn," although of course, because it is random, there is no "turn" or set sequence. While we cannot explain the magic of this exercise, it goes a long way toward getting a group in tune with one another.

The last step before moving on is to acknowledge and utilize physicality through a simple exercise. Each person pairs up with another person, preferably someone they barely, if at all, know. They spend time trying to figure out as many things as possible that they have in common, without speaking or vocalizing. Through only body language they focus on one another and create ideas and pictures. After stopping the experiment, perhaps they can give a rough count of things they have in common. Without words and solely through the use of body language, they begin to acknowledge the power and effectiveness of physicality.

III.

STORYTELLING: "ONCE UPON A TIME"

INTRODUCTION

Lawyers naturally and easily access storytelling skills every day in hallways, streets and bars. Unfortunately, the courtroom tends to bring out the worst in lawyers. They lose the precious "Once upon a time..." mentality they developed as young children and begin speaking "legalese." They lose the natural skills that make them effective communicators in "normal" situations and have difficulty translating those natural storytelling skills into powerful courtroom performance and persuasion.

Indeed, good trial lawyers are good storytellers, and most often, all other things being equal, the advocate telling the most powerful, compelling and persuasive *story* will win a trial. *Before* a trial begins, however, a lawyer must jump inside the client's story and tap into the best way to present the story at trial.

Like improv, storytelling is a topic worthy of books in its own right, and those books have been written. We focus on using improv to help lawyers intimately access a story, effectively craft and develop a story and persuasively present the story in court.

BACKBONE OF THE STORY: "ONCE UPON A TIME..."

"If you can't bring your story down to a logline or one page, it is a pretty good indication that you haven't found the core of your story." — Unknown

A lawyer's tendency to succumb to their legal training and the temptation to recite *facts* often interferes with their ability to translate their effective and natural "once upon a time" storytelling into the courtroom setting. This partially explains why most lawyers have seen, and many have been guilty of making, a closing argument ("summation") starting with, "Now let us review and recap the testimony of each witness...." Incidentally, one only imagines the thoughts of jurors (or judges) who have listened to weeks or months of testimony, as they think to themselves and plead with the lawyer, "I have heard the witnesses! Let's not!!"

Rather than carefully crafting effective stories, lawyers often take the easier, albeit far less persuasive option of delivering a basic factual recitation. While perhaps at times due to a lack of effort, it is often due to the lawyer's inability to recognize and access the backbone inherent in a story.

When considering the backbone of the story, we look at the story from start to finish. Admittedly, in some cases with clearly defined characters, plots and resolutions, the story backbone is readily apparent and easy to access. In many stories, lawyers easily recognize the beginning, middle and end of the story, which is not to say those three parts need be presented in that order. However, some fact patterns are not as easily accessible.

In deciphering why a story is eventually told and played out in court, we fairly assume that something went awry, and in some way, and for some known or unknown reason, there is a problem. Thus, all courtroom stories (and most stories) have a platform and a tilt.

The platform refers to day to day life as it exists for characters in a story and people generally. They go about their lives, whether remarkable or mundane, complicated or simple, relatively free of conflict, and with no unordinary problems. Their lives and the platform upon which they live is well established, offering them normal and reasonable expectations and daily experiences.

The tilt, then, is that point when some unusual and unordinary problem arises, most often the problem that brings the case to court. Life is somehow thrown into disarray and their platform tilts, causing their world to become skewed and disrupted in an unusual and most often unwelcome way. The fact that the unwelcome tilt brings the story to court explains why, with the exception of lawyers or other personnel paid to be in court, no one otherwise chooses to go to court.

Using a common, criminal case fact pattern without an obvious story backbone, we use one of our warm up exercises from above to get a better handle on the story backbone.

Assume you defend Mr. Smith in the following case. The police allege they saw him drop a small bag of narcotics in front of them, try to walk away and he was subsequently arrested. From the prosecution's perspective, the story is apparent and accessible. Two astute and well-trained young policemen are out on foot one evening serving and protecting the community. Using their training to ferret out crime, they see a "suspicious" looking Smith. As Smith looks in their direction, he drops a bag of suspect narcotics to the ground and the officers move in for the arrest. This story comes in a pretty package, ready to present to a jury.

Consider for a minute a possible story, or more accurately, lack thereof, in defending Smith. He did not drop any drugs as he walked down the street, and the police are not credible because..... End of story, period. Obviously, "He did not drop any drugs" is really not a story at all, but merely a lifeless, spineless statement, and at best, an emotionally vacant factual theory of defense.

So how do we get a grip on a real *story* to present at trial? We use the same storytelling formula from our warm ups to prompt a story from our facts. This time, however, we use the backbone in a case specific way:

"Once upon a time...
Every day...
But one day...
Because of that...
Because of that...
Because of that... (Repeat because of that
as often as needed to flush out story)
Until finally...
Ever since then...
The moral of the story is...."

By plugging in some facts from Smith's case, we start to create a true story and move beyond the overly simplistic and dry, "He did not drop any drugs." Incidentally, brainstorming cases in a group setting provides tremendous value and we use this exercise effectively with a group, with each person quickly adding to the story. If applied to our facts, it might go something like this:

Once upon a time there was a young man named William Smith who was a good high school student and diligent worker at Richardson's grocery store...

Every day, William would walk to the park after school to play basketball with his friends, before going to the store to do inventory for Mr. Richardson...

But one day, William walked to the park with some bad people he did not know well...

Because of that, some overly-aggressive police officers started following the group for no apparent reason...

Because of that, they believed William might be carrying drugs and zeroed in on William...

Because of that, the officers arrested William and took an innocent man to the police station...

Because of that, William was kicked out of school and lost his job...

Until finally, William realized his only choice was to have 12 jurors hear his case...

Ever since then, he has been waiting to tell those jurors he is innocent...

The moral of the story is, if you hang out with the wrong people, be ready to stand up for yourself in court.

Through the formula, we begin creating a platform and tilt *story*, with a beginning, middle and end, which again, is not to say we must present the story in that order at trial. We now begin to see the story backbone, platform and tilt. By continuing to brainstorm Smith's fact pattern using this backbone two or three more times, of course giving consideration to evidence we will actually adduce at trial, we begin to create a true story of innocence. We will bolster our story with themes and hook phrases.

This backbone prompt works well when a true story is difficult to decipher from "facts." But even in a case with a readily apparent and easily recognizable story, this backbone will quickly work out a story from start to finish in several different ways, offering a lawyer different and valuable options for presenting the case in court.

MICRO VIEW OF THE STORY: IMAGES, SENSES AND MEMORY

"You can actually end up telling a more universal story the more you really burrow into a specific world."

— Damien Chazelle

"I always considered myself a minor writer. My province is small, and I try to explore it very, very thoroughly."

— Leonard Cohen

PAINTING WORD PICTURES

After exploring and understanding the story backbone, we sift through important scenes and jump inside our characters' heads. However, first we move our focus from the macro view of the story to the far extreme - the micro view of the story.

Because legal training often focuses on facts rather than stories, many lawyers tend to broad stroke important, helpful facts of a case, rather than milking those helpful ideas to make a story more plausible and persuasive. In opening statement and closing argument, lawyers miss valuable opportunities to paint word pictures and frame their story around powerful and memorable images. Instead, they choose to broad stroke, often using *conclusory* language. On cross-examination, lawyers also tend to move directly toward conclusions rather than telling stories and creating images. Incidentally, facts appearing "collateral" to a story, when fleshed out, will often make jurors look more favorably on a client or character. We discuss this idea in more depth later.

First, we discuss an exercise for non case specific facts and rather mundane stories. We use the exercise to fully flesh out a story by painting descriptive word pictures and creating vivid "still" photo images. Then, as lawyers, we use this skill on cases according to our *theory* to highlight important parts of a story at trial through word pictures. Once mastered, this skill becomes an important part of a trial lawyer's repertoire.

To learn to effectively paint word pictures, imagine for a moment speaking with a friend on the phone while looking at a picture to which the friend is not privy. Your friend needs to know in *specific detail* what the photograph portrays, "facetime" does not exist and you must create that picture for your friend as descriptively and precisely as possible. As a skilled artist, your friend relies on your description to draw a likeness that approximates your image. The image they conjure up and draw should nearly replicate your image.

In court we need to ably and descriptively create for jurors an image they cannot and did not see. Like a persuasive storyteller, we skillfully stop a story, bring the plot to a halt, and meticulously paint word pictures. When done well and in support of our theory, these word pictures indelibly etch images into the minds and memory of jurors, making the story as a whole more plausible and powerful.

Powerful images have lasting effect. Thinking back to a good story, whether oral, written or on the screen, generally we have some memory of plot and dialogue. But most often, compelling images most indelibly etch into our memory while verbal content takes a backseat to those images. For instance, the plot of a movie like "The Deer Hunter," of a working-class community in Pennsylvania, likely does not stick with the viewer as long as the *images* of young men holding guns to their heads during "Russian Roulette."

Similarly, as we discuss later, emotional memory is greater than verbal memory. In the words of Maya Angelou, "People will forget what you did. People will forget what you said. But people will never forget how you made them *feel*."

Perhaps the left brain/right brain theory is a myth, and we will not belabor over a discussion and debate about which side lawyers use most. Yet, years of academic experiences, and law school in particular, can certainly de-condition many lawyers from effectively and comfortably accessing their brains in a creative way. Some lawyers function at times almost exclusively through the verbal and logical part of the brain, simultaneously shutting off the part of the brain that handles images, intuition and emotion.

We can, however, reclaim these creative instincts. After all, we easily access our creative minds as audience members of movies or readers of books. We need to rev up these instincts as storytellers, and more specifically, as word picture artists.

To refine our skills of painting word pictures and creating images, we use an exercise we call "Advance, Color, Emotion." This exercise is effective for brainstorming cases and courtroom storytelling alike.

The exercise works as follows. One person tells a story to an audience. While telling the story, a second person directs the storyteller with prompts of either "advance," "color," or "emotion." At the prompt of "advance," the storyteller moves the "plot" along and the story actually advances in time. Upon a prompt of "color," with the "color" prompt directed toward a specific part, fact or idea of the story ("Color your car...," for example, not referring specifically to the color of the car, of course, but rather to the car itself), the storyteller speaks only about "the car," until the director again says "advance," prompting the storyteller to again move the plot along. The storyteller's challenge and purpose is to describe the car by painting a graphic, vivid and fully detailed *word picture* of the car. A "color" prompt can indicate anything at all, whether it be animate, inanimate, a thought or feeling. After a word picture or vivid description, the director prompts the storyteller to "advance" the story, again moving the plot along.

Once the storyteller is comfortable painting word pictures, the director then works in the "emotion" prompt, signaling the storyteller to vividly and fully describe the emotion they, or a third party, feel at that particular time in the story. While we discuss emotional range later in greater detail, during this exercise lawyers start to acknowledge and explore the significance of emotions in a story.

To demonstrate this exercise, we first use an everyday, common event. Storyteller (S) tells the story of going to the grocery store while Director (D) "directs" the story.

S "This morning I walked into the grocery store and saw my friend Tom."

(D interrupts, prompting S to "color" Tom)

S continues, focusing solely on "Tom" until the next "advance" prompt, "Tom is five foot nine, with a medium build, dark brown hair, a thick goatee beard and small, round wire-rimmed glasses. He has a round face and a gap between his two upper middle teeth..."

(D interrupts with "advance", prompting S to move along the plot.)

S continues, "...After saying 'hi' to Tom, I walked to the left around the outside aisle of the store, over to the produce where they had all sorts of peppers..."

(D interrupts, prompting S to "color" all sorts of peppers.)

S continues, "...the peppers were laid out in a three foot deep by six foot wide area, divided equally by green colored dividers into six rectangular areas. The entire shelf of peppers leaned downward away from the wall about twenty degrees and in the front bin on the left there were jalapeno peppers..."

(D interrupts, prompting S to "color" the jalapeno peppers.)

S continues, "...there were about eighty to one hundred jalapeno peppers, most of which were green, though a few of them were reddish-green. They were mostly about three inches long and about one inch in diameter, and most of them were somewhat wilted and they were pretty expensive for what you were getting..."

(D interrupts, prompting S to "color" pretty expensive for what you were getting)

S continues, "...well, jalapenos at this particular store are usually seventy cents a pound, but they are usually fresh and not at all wilted, but these were one dollar and twenty cents a pound and they were wilted and scuffed-up..."

(D interrupts, prompting S to "advance.")

S continues, "...After looking at the peppers, I went to the bakery, where I ran into my old girlfriend, Susan..."

(D interrupts, prompting S's "emotion" as he saw his old girlfriend Susan)

S continues, coloring his emotion as he saw his old girlfriend Susan, "... I felt confused and embarrassed because we did not break up under the best of circumstances. I would have rather been anywhere but there! My insides froze up; I didn't know whether to say "hi" or keep walking, but I felt like I owed it to her to say something...."

The story continues while D directs S to paint word pictures, create images and fully flesh out his emotions. In this example, of course, the "color" prompts were without a specific purpose and not choreographed, but rather to demonstrate the technique.

This exercise works well with a partner but can also be used alone to develop the skill of stopping a story at a moment's notice, focusing on a particular fact or idea and painting word pictures.

While preparing and brainstorming cases this exercise will fully flesh out and milk important parts of the story, including emotions, to make the story more powerful. After deciding which areas to flesh out, we run our "Advance-color-emotion" technique throughout an entire story, using it as a maximizing button at trial to freeze and highlight important facts that support our case theory.

Many years ago we used this exercise with a colleague who was at best skeptical. After he crafted a story for opening statement, we discussed "Advance, Color, Emotion," and we used the exercise on a non-case related, otherwise mundane story. He was somewhat interested, a bit entertained and slightly amused, yet still skeptical, rightfully wanting to know how it applied to persuading jurors.

We discussed a DUI client and he delivered a sample opening statement that he felt told his client's story. His sample opening went something like this, with names changed, of course, to protect the innocent:

"On the night of April 9, 1999, at about eleven p.m., Mr. Sean Murphy, left work at O'Sullivan's restaurant, exhausted, and headed home. As he drove his car home, he was pulled over by a State Trooper, who ordered him out of the car. Mr. Murphy got out of the car and turned around to face the direction of the trooper's car. Mr. Murphy did not know what to do so he opened his wallet to take out his license...," and the story went on for another couple of minutes.

With some understanding of the story, we directed the story using the "Advance, Color, Emotion" technique, and he told the story as planned, with the interjected "advance," "color" and "emotion" prompts.

His opening statement then went something like this, with the letters A, C and E indicating the prompts:

> "On the night of April 9, 1999, at about eleven p.m., Mr. Sean Murphy left work. (C on "work at the restaurant"). Mr. Murphy worked, as he had for years, as a musician in a traditional Irish band. He played the traditional fiddle with five other musicians. That night he played from four p.m. until about ten-thirty p.m., at Slainte, a traditional Irish restaurant that catered primarily to families. Mr. Murphy spent the night skillfully playing traditional Irish songs. (C on "skillfully playing"). Playing Irish music involves focus and skill, as the tempo varies from fast to slow, and the players have to be on time with their notes at all times. If you miss a note, particularly on the fiddle, which is the driving force of the music, it would be punishing on the ears. (A) When Mr. Murphy left work, he headed home to see his wife and two daughters, because he was exhausted. (C on "exhausted"). Mr. Murphy could barely keep his eyes open. He had woken up early that morning to feed his daughters breakfast, and then worked an 8 hour shift at the grocery store. For the previous six and one-half hours, with only one fifteen minute break, he had been focused intently on playing his fiddle. (A) As he drove down expressway 290 to get home, he saw the flashing lights of a police car behind him. (E when he saw the flashing lights). He was confused, knowing he had not done anything wrong. His emotion turned to disappointment, as he thought about his sole desire – to get home as soon as possible to see his wife and

daughters. He then, became angry, knowing he had done nothing wrong and would have rather been anywhere else..."

After experimenting for a few more minutes with the exercise, we stopped to discuss how the story changed and why the new, revised version would be more persuasive in court. The lawyer recognized that the first sentence of his opening developed significantly, took on new meaning and added several things that would convince the jury. By pressing the "maximizing" button on a few basic things during a small snippet of the story, his client and the story took on a whole new look.

Parenthetically, he also recognized and utilized another storytelling technique, noting that sometimes small facts of a story, seemingly collateral and unrelated to the trial issues, make a case stronger and more persuasive. While milking the story, he *humanized* Murphy by revealing to jurors Murphy's status as a likable, hard-working musician and caring parent and family man. Do these facts reflect anything about his sobriety or driving? Of course not. Might they give jurors reason to like him? Of course. If the jury likes him is he more likely to win the trial? Certainly, because they see him as a hardworking musician and father.

But here, the new and improved story did more to support the DUI defense than simply using apparently collateral facts meaningfully and productively. Murphy's dexterity and physical ability to play his instrument perhaps bears directly on his sobriety. His exhaustion, due to an unarguably long day and night, explains why the trooper believed he was drunk.

In addition to preparing the story for trial, this exercise does three things to prepare a witness' direct-examination testimony. First, the lawyer ensures before trial that the witness thinks through and fleshes out all of the possible topics that might arise. It will get Murphy, for instance, to think about things he might otherwise deem unimportant to his case. Second, a witness will practice *verbalizing* and describing important and relevant parts of the story for direct examination. And third, some witnesses, while using this technique, will actually interject important facts unknown to the lawyer.

The temptation to broad stroke over important facts commonly exists on cross examination. While telling stories on cross examination, albeit fragmented stories, lawyers often try enticing witnesses to acknowledge conclusions. Unfortunately, witnesses seldom admit to conclusions, particularly subjective conclusions. For example, the lawyer broad strokes by using the word "drunk" and the witness adamantly denies being drunk. Using the "color" tool on the word "drunk," where the witness was undoubtedly inebriated, the lawyer proves and demonstrates the point with images of the witness drinking in the bar, describing the bar, drinks, behavior and scene.

The "Advance, Color, Emotion" technique aids brainstorming cases by breaking down the story, recognizing supportive images and choreographing those images skillfully in support of the theory. With a mastered ability to flesh out ideas and create word pictures at a moments' notice, lawyers confidently know the "maximizing" button is always available.

Developing The Story Through Transitions, Scenes And "Stills"

INTRODUCTION

To persuasively present a story, we break up the story into scenes by emphasizing and "coloring" the critical scenes we want jurors to focus on and remember. Like a good movie director, we use effective transitions and change the pace of a story by slowing it down, speeding it up or simply bringing it to a halt by stopping the story and focusing on a "still" picture.

TRANSITIONS

To effectively transition in and out of different topics and scenes in court, we clearly delineate and make obvious for jurors *when* the transition occurs, so they recognize and *feel* the change. By using transitions in voir dire, opening statement, cross-examination, direct examination and closing argument, we keep jurors' attention, make our presentation easy to digest, and, hopefully, we let jurors recognize when something important is on the horizon. Like a drum roll, strategic and successful transitions persuade by gathering the jurors' undivided attention to important parts of our case.

When persuading jurors through a story, we recognize that some facts are inevitably more important than others. An entire story without transitions typically melts into one large blob, and unfortunately, jurors sense that all facts are equal because no parts of the story stand out. We want to strategically emphasize specific scenes, or other facts, to make the story most persuasive. Jurors will not, however, digest it as intended without transitions. Rather, all the scenes meld together as the story runs continuously. To make matters worse, at times lawyers use a monotone voice. The lack of transitions, or ineffective transitions at best, causes the blob story.

Transitions are noteworthy, if not remarkable, in music. Even without musical ability, a casual listener recognizes, consciously or otherwise, musical transitions. Most popular music contains a verse, chorus and bridge. Transitions effectively connect these three parts and bring the listener from one part of the song to the next. The transitions train listeners to expect each new part and listeners ready themselves as the different parts unfold. A typical "one-four-five" blues pattern is simple but has the same effect. Just as musicians transition to prepare us for different parts of a song, in court we should adeptly and effectively transition to clearly signal a shift in gear to jurors.

Mindful that all transitions are not equal, we use more significant transitions to introduce ideas critical to our case, and lesser transitions to simply switch topics while making our presentation more palatable and easier to digest. We recognize this difference because we should not constantly follow up a long drum roll with insignificant crumbs of information, thereby desensitizing the jury to what we are doing.

Obviously, we can transition through our use of language. We begin a series of questions, for instance, during voir dire or direct examination, with a phrase such as, "Let me ask you some questions *now* about...." Through language, which is perhaps the most common method of signaling a transition, jurors instantly know something new is on the horizon. In addition to language, or perhaps by using something in *combination with* language, how else can we signal a transition to jurors? Several things, used alone or in combination, will do the trick.

PAUSING AND SILENCE

While often undervalued and underutilized, a communicative pause and the accompanying silence, are a powerful and persuasive communicative device, particularly when used as a natural transition. Traditional lawyering promotes and exalts effective speaking. Lawyers too often view themselves as "winning" only when they are actually speaking, and somehow losing the battle when they become silent. Young lawyers in particular often completely eschew the idea of silence. They want to jump into the fray, which most often means speaking. They tend to avoid pauses, viewing them as a sign of weakness or surrender, perhaps because of the uncomfortable, accompanying silence.

To the speaker, silence feels uncomfortable for several reasons. Many speakers assume silence will waste valuable speaking time. Others find discomfort with the anomaly that they should be speaking, but find themselves standing silently while a group of people, whether twelve jurors or some other audience, stares at them, waiting on the next word. This feeling can be daunting. In any event, speakers probably feel unease during a pause because they have never considered silence from the *listener's* point of view.

Indeed, the persuasive value of a pause and the accompanying silence are recognized and appreciated from the listener's point of view. To listeners, a pause is most always welcome as it offers free time to digest and reflect upon a presentation. Listeners use the time productively to reflect on and digest material and to prepare for what is yet to come. Admittedly, given the increasingly shorter attention spans of audiences, due in large part to television and social media culture, it also, at times, offers a brief respite for their minds to wander off.

Legendary trumpeter Miles Davis, known by many as "The Prince of Silence," had a beautiful and undeniably distinct sound to his notes. When asked what made his notes sound so special, he said, to paraphrase, it was the silence before and the silence after. He used silence in his music as an art form, once telling another jazz legend, John Coltrane, that in order to play less, Coltrane had to take the "saxophone out of his mouth." When another band mate decided that a song sounded good and thus, started soloing, Davis instructed that the song sounded so good *because* the band mate was not playing. In each case the "Prince of Silence" emphatically noted that the power of silence must be appreciated, respected and utilized to the fullest to further his art. Indeed, Davis also used silence tremendously in his own solos.

Effective speakers welcome and find comfort in silence. They exude confidence as they pause. Their pauses, among the strongest weapons in their arsenal, are often used as transitions. Standing alone, a purposeful and artful pause naturally signals movement into new terrain. Used in conjunction with other transitional techniques, silence is a great "go to" tool as we effectively transition in the courtroom.

ALTERNATING VOLUME

Beyond a simple pause, other communicative tools effectively signal a transition, including the volume of our voice. Through a vast array of changing volumes, we create or highlight a transition, starting with a barely audible whisper, and gradually increasing incrementally to a louder voice.

Let's talk first about how to develop and refine our use of volume, and then talk about using volume effectively as a transition. By shifting and alternating volume to enhance courtroom presentations, we explore how different volume levels can highlight different parts of a story, depending on the content of each part of a story. In the courtroom, we seldom, if ever scream at the top of our lungs. We will at times, however, lower our voice to a near whisper.

The notion that a louder voice most effectively and appropriately gathers attention in court is not entirely true. In fact, a loud courtroom voice is often inappropriate. A near whisper more effectively causes jurors to lean in and pay close attention. Specifically, we notice in court how a change in volume from a normal voice to a near whisper usually has a mesmerizing effect, imploring jurors to listen attentively. This results largely from the juxtaposition of the different volumes.

While the shift to a whisper is perhaps most effective, any significant change in volume has a similar effect, and lawyers should practice alternating volumes. We learn to adjust volume in congruity with our presentation by using different volumes appropriately for different parts of a story.

To practice the juxtaposition of volume, imagine a scale of one to ten. The one represents a barely audible whisper, the five a normal speaking volume and the ten a near, all-out scream.

1	2	3	4	5	6	7	8	9	**10**

Near whisper..... Increasing volume.....Normal volume.....Increasing volume.....**Loud!!!!**

A director stands in the audience to give hand signals ranging from one to ten as a lawyer practices an opening statement. The speaker follows suit and adjusts volume accordingly. This causes the speaker to access several different volumes. In the process, particularly from the standpoint of the audience, we recognize the effectiveness of the change in volume. The seven to ten range are most often inappropriate for court, but the one through six are effective, particularly when moving more than one or two notches at a time.

Building on this idea of juxtaposing different volumes, we use volume to transition. Specifically, the juxtaposition between two different volumes grabs the jury's attention while also creating an effective transition. The juxtaposition delineates and makes obvious for jurors that a transition is occurring and we then move into new terrain. Used alone, a volume change serves as an effective transition. Used in combination with either triggering language or a pause, it is even more successful.

ALTERNATING TONE

Another voice activated tool used to trigger a transition is a change in tone. Different tones or inflections can signify a specific attitude, mood or emotion. Like a volume change, a change in tone effectively signals a transition to jurors, particularly when the change creates a clear and markedly distinguishable juxtaposition.

In communication generally, and in particular, storytelling, tone must be altered. A monotone presentation is boring, lifeless and sure to put an audience to sleep. A presentation lacking tonal variety, even an otherwise good presentation with good material, will usually fail. Lawyers need to interject life into presentations by varying tone. This variation makes stories more palatable, enjoyable and entertaining.

To understand tonal change used as an effective transition we go back to when we were children. We sat at the dinner table with a parent shortly after receiving a less than satisfactory report card. The dinner conversation was smooth as we discussed relatively mundane things like weather and t-ball. The parent's tone was happy and we sat comfortably because the topics, and more importantly, the conversational *tone* allowed us to relax. It was not threatening, nor did it put us back on our heels. Then (and incidentally often after a pause), our parent said with a tone that changed noticeably to stern and disappointed, "there is *something* we need to talk about." We did not know what we needed to talk about, but in addition to the verbal transition, it was more so the tone that clearly signaled a change in topic.

In the courtroom we use similar changes in tone as a transitional device. By simply shifting tones, we can signal to the jurors a movement to a different topic. For example, in the case of William Smith, we might use a somewhat "matter of fact" tone while discussing his ride to the station in the police car. However, a clearly noticeable change in tone will define and delineate other important scenes, when we want the jurors to know and *feel* our transition. With an unmistakable change in tone, we say, "But then William got to the station..." As we do so, we signal a transition to the jurors, grab their attention and more importantly, let them know that this part of the story is important.

All transitions are not equal just as all the facts and parts to a story are not equal. With this in mind, and according to our theory, we transition to convey to jurors a sense of immediacy and importance for certain parts of a case. For some parts, we will use the most distinguishable and effective transitions. These usually include a combination of two or more of our transitional techniques: language, silence, volume, tone or movement.

Some parts of a case, though not critical, are still worthy of a transition, albeit not a greatly impactful transition. We do not want to create a "boy who cried wolf" situation where transitions lose effect. Jurors will then view well-orchestrated transitions as a tease. They realize that every part of the case cannot be terribly important enough to warrant a major drum roll. The drum roll preceding relatively insignificant parts of the story will dilute others, and the transitions will eventually lose their effect entirely.

There are yet other, more subtle ways of transitioning, involving less fanfare. We can change our rhythm, pace or body language to create a transition, as long as the change is distinguishable. We can also use simple but distinct movements in the courtroom, a topic discussed later in more detail, to effectively transition. By noticeably turning around, facing a different direction or moving to a different area of the courtroom, especially in conjunction with a pause, we can clearly signal a transition to jurors.

SCENES

After moving from the backbone of our story, we break up the story into smaller increments to delineate important scenes that support our theory. Within those scenes, we might often stop the "video" to focus the jurors' attention on "still" photos and paint word pictures, often of objects or people we want to highlight within the scene. Our "Advance-Color-Emotion" tool descriptively creates both scenes and "stills."

We use a transition to set scenes and create a boundary for each scene. Among other things, we delineate the time and location of each scene for jurors. Because our theory dictates that we emphasize certain scenes, the scenes we want to stand out in the jurors' memory should be powerfully presented and well-delineated. Jurors must recognize that those scenes are significant to our story.

To prepare and create the scenes of our story for court, we imagine videotaping each scene to view how each scene unfolded. To descriptively create and develop scenes in court, we use the same precision and detail we used with our "color" tool to describe a photograph to a friend on the other end of the phone. Assuming our friend on the phone cannot see the scene, we create, as graphically as possible, a video for that person.

Incidentally, while we are obviously not directly and truly privy before trial to how exactly a scene unfolded (unless, of course there is a real video), our imaginary camera helps us begin to envision at least the *possibilities* of what happened.

For example, in Mr. Murphy's story we look at some important scenes and consider their significance. Then we decide which "stills" to "color" using our "Advance-Color-Emotion" technique.

Two of the important scenes of Mr. Murphy's case might be as follows:

1) Slainte Restaurant. Ironically, although it is a DUI case, we can humanize Murphy, showing him to be a working man and musician, and hopefully, also demonstrate his sobriety, given his ability to perform intricately on a musical instrument.
2) The scene on the highway where he was pulled over demonstrates the pressures he was under and the difficult physical conditions that existed when he performed field sobriety tests.

We introduce these critical scenes with a transition and flush them out using our "Advance-Color-Emotion" technique.

"STILLS"

Considering some useful "stills" from the above scenes, we use our "Advance-Color-Emotion" technique to create memorable images that stick in the jurors' heads. To descriptively create "stills," it is helpful to close our eyes, envision the "still" and lock that image in our head. Using the video technique to run through scenes, we stop the video at different points and look at a "still," just as we might take and print a "still" picture from a home video.

From Slainte Restaurant, for instance, we snap a shot of the band playing. Then through a word picture we graphically describe their set up to create an image for the jurors of Murphy working his craft. From the side of the highway, we take a "still" of Murphy standing by the side of the major highway with the police "mars" headlights spinning and a spotlight relentlessly shining in his face. We also take a "still" of Murphy sitting in the police station while seated on a metal bench and cuffed to a ringlet attached to the wall. Though unable to move comfortably, he asserts his innocence to anyone that will listen.

We naturally and most obviously think of creating persuasive scenes and "stills" during opening statement or closing argument because of the storytelling format of these two areas of a trial. However, we also utilize this concept on direct and cross-examination.

As a witness tells their story on direct examination, we prepare the testimony by highlighting specific scenes and "stills" supportive of our theory. Using the "Advance-Color-Emotion" technique, we ensure that the witness fully and effectively fleshes out their story. Incidentally, preparing a witness' testimony using this technique helps aid them in understanding the important parts of their story.

We also use simple, "once upon a time" storytelling during cross-examination to create scenes and "stills." Unfortunately lawyers often overlook the storytelling aspect of cross examination. They anticipate only the confrontational communication between two people from different sides of a case, with each person trying to get the better of the other person.

Good cross-examination, however, is true storytelling. Starting with the unstated, but igniting "once upon a time" phrase, an effective cross examiner tells a story through opposing witnesses, even though those witnesses are often hostile. During cross-examination we tell a *fragmented* story, because the witness will methodically answer with a simple "yes," or "no," as desired, thus, fragmenting our story. As the cross examiner narrates, however, the jury will listen to and digest the thread created by the examiner rather than the "yes" answers.

Using storytelling tools during cross-examination, we create scenes and "stills" to enhance the story. During our cross examination of the police officer, for instance, we focus on and set up a scene, together with an accompanying "still," of Murphy standing by the side of the road.

Q – (Verbal transition) I want to ask you some questions about what happened after your car pulled over, you understand

A – Yes

Q – Your car was parked

A – Yes

Q – On the west side of the road

A – Yes

Q – Behind Mr. Murphy's car

A – Yes

Q – About five feet behind his car

A – Yes

Q – With both cars facing southbound

A – Yes

Q – You got out of your car

A – Yes

Q – You looked at Mr. Murphy

A – Yes

Q – He stood by his car

A – Yes

Q – Facing you

A – Yes

Q – Facing your car

A – Yes

Q – You were next to Highway 61

A – Yes

Q – There was traffic moving by you

A – Yes

Q – It was loud

A – Yes

Q – Mr. Murphy stood within six feet of the nearest lane of traffic

A – Yes

(Now we stop the video and take a "still" photo, essentially painting a word picture, or image, of Mr. Murphy standing by the roadside, with some of the concepts supportive of our theory.)

Q – Mr. Murphy stood there

A – Yes

Q – By the side of Highway 61

A – Yes

Q – Within six feet of the nearest lane

A – Yes

Q – There were lights on Mr. Murphy

A – Yes

Q – Overhead street lights

A – Yes

Q – A spotlight

A – Yes

Q – From your car

A – Yes

Q – And spinning mars lights

A – Yes

Q – From your car

A – Yes

Q – And headlights

A – Yes

Q – Also from your car

A – Yes

Q – He was well illuminated (Of course we don't say "well lit up," given the nature of the charge!)

A – Yes

Q – He was wearing a cap

A – Yes

Q – Made of wool

A – Yes

Q – He wore a shirt

A – Yes

Q – A button down shirt

A – Yes

Q – It was tucked in

A – Yes

Q – He did not sway

A – No

Q – He did not slump

A – No

(To learn more about effective cross examination, please see "MacCarthy on Cross Examination.")

By creating and presenting both a scene and a "still" photograph initially in opening statement and now on cross examination, we set the table for the closing argument, when we will again present the scene in great depth, and argumentatively explain its significance to the jurors. Moreover, we implanted a lasting *image* of Mr. Murphy in jurors' minds that they will use to understand his theory and story.

Before wrapping up this chapter, we digress briefly to note the importance of using a story by analogy in a closing argument. A frequently used, albeit basic example, is how we go to bed with no snow on the ground, fall asleep and wake to see snow. By analogy, this story does some of our heavy lifting by *explaining* circumstantial evidence.

We utilize all of the storytelling techniques discussed above when we persuade during a closing argument with a story by analogy. Though the facts of the analogy are separate and distinct from the facts of our case, we use the analogy to persuade. The story by analogy, when used properly, immediately and without explanation promotes our theory and helps jurors understand our case.

IV.

STATUS AND ROLES

INTRODUCTION

In the home, street, or workplace, people constantly judge and treat others according to status and roles ("status"). Status constantly and pervasively impacts, and in many instances dictates, communication on many levels. It is intertwined with and inseparable from communication. Although we perhaps only admit reluctantly, ("Not me! I treat all people with the same amount of respect and dignity!"), we constantly send and read communication signals affected by status. Of course some people do treat all people, regardless of status, with dignity and respect. That is not to say, however, that their communication is unaffected and uninfluenced by the complex influence of status. Status likewise impacts and inundates storytelling and the always changing set of courtroom relationships.

Incidentally, status also pervasively infiltrates the animal kingdom. It acknowledges certain creatures as high status and often punishes those who do not respect and abide by the system. Without discussing the animal kingdom's unique system of status, we note that some of the same concepts apply to and are analogous with the courtroom.

The way courtroom relationships play out can and sometimes will be the difference between winning and losing a trial. A good trial lawyer recognizes and understands how status affects the courtroom and adjusts communication, where possible, to take advantage of this dynamic during a trial. On cross examination, for instance, we typically avoid honorifics ("Mr.", "Ms.", "Detective," etc.) because those honorifics elevate the status of our opponent's witnesses. The opposite, of course, is also true. We want to use honorifics, usually on direct examination, when we seek to elevate a witness' status. How can we use status beneficially in general and how can we elevate the status of different players in a trial to benefit our case?

The exploration of status in improv is significant. (In his groundbreaking book "IMPRO: IMPROVISATION AND THE THEATRE," Keith Johnstone is credited with exploring and emphasizing the importance of status in improv.) We will discuss that exploration and then discuss its pertinence to trial lawyers, the courtroom and storytelling.

STATUS AND ROLES: A CHANGING FACTOR, A CONSTANT REMINDER

For better or worse and right or wrong, status permeates and is inseparable from all communication. A person's status ranges in a spectrum from high to low and anywhere in between. In a hotel setting, for instance, whether hotel manager, owner or bellman, valet or bartender, front desk worker or maid, status constantly affects communication.

Status uniquely depends on a particular "setting" and often changes, as a new setting often dictates changes in status. At times, the change in setting causes an unexpected and quick change in status.

For instance, a judge who holds a relatively high status at work, particularly in court, might hold a significantly lesser status as she walks home from work on the street, and yet an even lower status when she walks into her house to greet her teenage daughters. Most of her communication, including attitudes, comments and expressions, likely changes as she makes her way from the courtroom to her home.

STATUS AND ROLES: THE CARD GAME

Lawyers explore status through improv in order to understand its pertinence to storytelling and how best to use it successfully to their benefit in court. We focus on a fun, simple status exercise to illuminate its significance.

Use this exercise after everyone warms up, and more importantly, after they have internalized the art of accepting the offer.

For lack of a better name, we will call this the card game and the exercise goes like this. A group assembles and each person is given a playing card to hold up to their forehead, with the card facing outward and visible to the rest of the group. Each person, however, must *not* look at the value of their own card. Players use cards ranging from a two to an ace, at times with extra high and low end cards in the mix to create and demonstrate more status disparity. The ace is high and the two, low. The ace, for instance, represents the CEO or other prominent person in a company, and the lower cards represent workers of far lesser "importance" to the company.

The players then improvise a scene where they attend an annual company holiday party or other annual, company function. The players interact in the meeting by treating other players according to the value of the playing card on each person's forehead, remembering not to look at their own card and *not* to make obvious "giveaway" comments revealing what each person represents, such as "...You are fit to be a king!...," or "you are really a jack of all trades...." The exercise develops as the players mingle at the party for several minutes or until such time as most all of the participants have a chance to interact with one another, all the while treating each other according to their number in the pecking order.

After sufficient mingling and interacting, usually several minutes, the game is halted. The participants are instructed to refrain from looking at their own card, and *without doing so*, line up in order based on how they felt they were treated in terms of importance. They can of course look at others' cards while choosing a place in line. Generally, most line ups very closely, and at times exactly, reflect the pecking order established by the playing cards. The aces and face cards will be on one end, the twos and threes on the other, and the middle cards, usually in relatively appropriate order, in the middle.

Once the participants establish their place in line, they can then look at the value of their own cards before a debriefing about the experience. How were they treated and how did it feel? How did it feel to be on the high end? Why? How did it feel to be in the middle or the low end? Why? What were the verbal and nonverbal signals they received? Did they feel comfortable? Why or why not? What specific signals guided them in determining their place in the line without looking at their own cards?

It will not be unreasonable or unexpected for a lawyer to ask what this has to do with the courtroom. This leads naturally to a discussion about the courtroom and a deeper analysis of the complex web of courtroom relationships. From the bailiff to the judge, the witness to the lawyer, the court reporter to the client, where does everyone stand and why? Where should everyone stand for a winning result? How can we elevate status where necessary?

THE "STATUS" OF BEING A LAWYER

Lawyers generally, and to a greater extent trial lawyers, are not known for having small egos. Perhaps that is an unfair "bad rap." However, to the extent the reputation holds true, some trial lawyers do have difficulty imagining themselves as anything but high status. They regularly expect "ace," or at a minimum "face card," treatment. Feeling the status of a "low" card offers a new, eye opening experience, if not a rude awakening.

Many people who view themselves as holding high status commonly and comfortably speak down to others. Inevitably, the speaker looks bad. This behavior and attitude obviously works to a lawyer's detriment in court, particularly in the jurors' eyes. Experiencing low status, even in a make-believe setting, gives some lawyers pause, helping them develop a greater and more meaningful sense of empathy.

On a positive note, many trial lawyers are kind, gracious and yes, dare we say, humble human beings. This group will use the card game to expose and explore the effect of status on human interaction and behavior, shedding light on how and why we treat other people the way we do.

Beyond a lawyers' view of their own status, we consider their status in the jurors' eyes. Based on experience and reputation, jurors do not necessarily view lawyers as having high status. Lawyers however, can positively or negatively enhance their status, whether deliberately or not, through a whole array of communicative tools, including language and body language.

For instance, we can affect our courtroom status, for better or worse, through eye-contact. Some lawyers attempt to establish dominant status by overemphasizing eye contact and "staring down" jurors. Typically this is not successful or effective. The opposite can be true as well, as some lawyers shy away from eye-contact, creating and acknowledging their own low status. We cover eye contact in more depth in chapter IX.

A lawyer's movement in court also sends clear status signals to others. When speaking, do they cower behind counsel table or a lectern, sending low status signals, or do they confidently move to the center of the courtroom to elevate their status? Lawyers constantly stake out territory in the courtroom, from counsel table to the bench, from lectern to witness box, attempting to establish high status, similar to neighborhood turf. Some relatively neutral areas are claimed and reclaimed. The courtroom starts as an empty canvas and develops into a caged chess board with each side fighting for territory, and sometimes snarling at those that tread in unwelcome territory.

This partially explains a lawyer's defensive feeling when opposing counsel circles their counsel table. If you doubt this concept, stand behind your opponent at their counsel table while trying a case and wait for the inevitable look that will kill. Better yet, remember your feelings when opposing counsel returned the favor and did this to you.

A lawyer's instinct and inclination may well be to constantly create high status and become an ace. However, it is debatable whether this high status is *always* most effective during a trial, because as we will see in a minute, the better practice often is to defer and let the jurors hold ace status. Perhaps we at times let the judge hold high status by quoting her.

Does our desire to take on the role of the ace sometimes detract from that goal? Might the courtroom run out of room, figuratively speaking, for so many people of high status? Do we run the risk of frightening off jurors? The answer to all three questions is probably "yes."

We certainly do not want to cower in a corner and refuse to make eye contact, but there are certain things we might tone down somewhat communicatively when we recognize that our attempt to become an ace might not always help our case or give us the best chance of winning a trial. We associate high status with competency, preparedness, being in control and a lack of nerves. Yet some lawyers are effective and successful while exhibiting signs of lower status, such as stumbling or mispronouncing words. Not every jury reacts well to a polished Wall Street lawyer. When we inevitably stumble in court, our response is telling. We keep our chin up and always look like we are winning. In the jurors' minds, we are doing a good job and fighting for our client.

COLLIDING PERSONALITIES: THE A AND B GAME

Through another exercise we explore and demonstrate why, whether in court or in normal conversation, we might not always want to be an ace. The exercise goes like this. We divide a room of people into two groups. On the right we have the "A" group, and on the left we have the "B" group. The groups prepare to meet in a business meeting similar to the card game meeting, but this time, rather than holding cards, the "A" group behaves as extroverts in an over-the-top, bordering on obnoxious manner. They are outgoing, gregarious and lively. They welcome conversation and always insist on eye contact and physical contact including hugs or lingering, firm handshakes. The "B" group on the other hand behaves as introverts in an over the top manner. They are shy, reluctant to make eye contact and very uneasy at the thought of any physical contact. The groups collide in the middle of the room and socialize, or socialize as best they can, for a few minutes. After several minutes, the groups switch roles and repeat the process.

This exercise gives lawyers the chance to extend themselves in two opposite directions. Hopefully, while neither role suits them perfectly, they will find their own, appropriate comfort level. Many, of course, customarily act more like the "A" group, which identifies more consistently with a trial lawyer's personality.

Perhaps a greater benefit of the exercise is the lawyer's experience with both types of personalities and the valuable first hand look from two ends of the spectrum. The "A" group's attempt to maintain the highest status is not all it is cracked up to be and borderline obnoxious. It is oblivious to its effect on other people. Unfortunately, some lawyers are those "A" people in the courtroom and they likewise are oblivious to their effect on others, especially jurors.

Accomplished trial lawyers do not constantly strive for ace status. They shelve their egos and any attempts to raise their own status are done artfully and effectively for a greater good and of course consistent with their case theory. They want to win the case. They might be a "ten," but that status leaves room for twelve aces in the jury box.

THE INTRICATE WEB OF COURTROOM RELATIONSHIPS

Courtroom relationships are complex and ever-changing. Three questions beg, based on the card game experiment. What status does everyone in the courtroom hold? If you have a choice, what status would they hold? And lastly, if you are displeased with the existing hierarchy, what can you do to change it?

The first question is the most difficult. Perhaps the only thing lawyers agree upon is that the jurors should sit as aces, or certainly high face cards. While the extent to which we raise the jurors' status is done fluidly and on a case by case basis, we acknowledge that when we complete the evidence and arguments and the judge instructs the jurors, they alone decide your client's fate. Whether freedom, money or actual life is in the balance, we cater to and obey the jurors because, with a few limited legal exceptions, they have the final say.

We do not advocate phony and superficial attempts to become chummy with jurors. Yet, in the front of our minds the jurors' sensibilities serve as *the* guiding light for everything we do in court, including every question, objection, argument, movement and attitude. We never talk down to jurors, nor do we bore, annoy or offend the jury. We also know to present a persuasive, memorable and hopefully, dare we say, entertaining case. With very few "always" and "never" rules in trial advocacy, a lawyer who questions a trial tactic, how to proceed or what to do need only consider their case theory and ask: How will the jurors look at this and will this help me persuade them? In this way, jurors are and should be aces in the courtroom.

The existing hierarchy for everyone else in the courtroom depends of course on whose eyes make the determination. Your eyes likely place your client high on the list. The more important question, though, is how your client can gain high status in the eyes of others in court, in particular the jurors. Beyond jurors, we consider other sets of eyes: the judge, your opponent at counsel table, the bailiff, clerk and court reporter.

Is it crazy to consider the opinion of the bailiff, clerk and court reporter? Not at all. All of them constantly sit in front of the jurors, and like everyone else in court, they continuously, consciously or subconsciously, send overt signals to jurors and others around them, including your client. A bailiff in a criminal case who treats the accused with decency and respect sends a positive message to jurors that can help raise the accused's status and potentially help the cause.

From the jurors' point of view, what hierarchy exists and how do they make that determination? Perhaps they defer to the judge. They are impressed by and respectful of her. After all, the judge greeted them and welcomed them to court. She kindly conversed with them at the beginning of the case, and in particular, during voir dire she established rapport with them. So, unless the judge bored or offended the jurors, she might be the ace in their eyes.

During voir dire, the potential jurors' experiences and values, rather than stereotypes based on race, ethnicity or gender, reveal the most about their suitability to hear a case. Likewise, jurors' experiences and values most significantly influence their determination of the courtroom status hierarchy. Thus, we focus on experiences and values rather than stereotypes.

Jurors infatuated with popular culture's courtroom drama and "real life" court television might highly regard lawyers, viewing them as intriguing, interesting or entertaining. Others, perhaps due to a bad past experience in our legal system, might subscribe to the poor reputation, whether deserved or not, lawyers sometimes hold in our society. To this latter group, lawyers probably fall in the second to last credibility spot, behind politicians.

The type of case presented might further influence the lawyer's status in the jurors' eyes. Does a juror highly regard a prosecutor because they represent "The People" and everything "good" associated with our society? Does a juror have negative experiences with our criminal justice system involving police misconduct, planting evidence or innocent people going to jail? Might we not benefit in defending a criminal case by accusing the government of being too high status as we argue that "my client's life and liberty are not important enough for the government to prove all the elements?" Does a juror consider the criminal defense lawyer as someone who is only in court because they were "appointed" and have no choice but to give a bad guy a "day in court"? Does the lawyer represent little Bobby Walker, a Little League World Series pitcher and aspiring symphony violinist, who lost his right hand in an allegedly malfunctioning ice cream truck refrigerator owned by the "Mega Ice Cream Company" and their billion dollar insurance company? Are we seeking anger, justice or mercy? Our case theory dictates how we use status as a tool.

This discussion does not provide all the answers, but lawyers need to consider status in the courtroom and where desirable, how they can raise the status of jurors, themselves, their clients and witnesses.

VOIR DIRE AND DELIBERATIONS: WHO'S RUNNING THE SHOW?

All lawyers and trial advocacy professors opine about the single most critical and important part of a trial. Many argue that opening statement is most important because you can actually win or lose during an opening. Regardless of opinion, most agree that voir dire is at or near the top of the list because during voir dire, lawyers question the venire and then make critical decisions by selecting the twelve people who will determine the client's fate. Some federal courtrooms, where attorney conducted voir dire is not favored, might be an exception.

Parenthetically, the traditional goals of voir dire, including educating the jurors and creating rapport, should be simplified. We really seek out the twelve people who are best suited to hear and most likely to *accept our client's story*. This simplified goal provides the guiding light to any questions or issues that arise during voir dire, including decisions about accepting or striking jurors.

Because status permeates voir dire and jury deliberations, we will discuss the two subjects in terms of how our improv exploration into status sheds light on each subject with a view toward better outcomes at trial.

VOIR DIRE

Voir dire provides a unique opportunity to elevate the jurors' status and lawyers should take full advantage. While potential jurors reluctantly find themselves in an unfamiliar, overly-formal and at times intimidating setting, lawyers should quickly and at every turn elevate the jurors' status. This of course inherently conflicts somewhat with a lawyer's goal of running the show during trial. As lawyers puff out their chests in several ways to run the courtroom, their tactics often inhibit their attempts at raising the jurors' status.

Voir dire by its nature is about *sharing* information on one level, and more specifically, eliciting information from potential jurors, including beliefs, stories, experiences and values. The gold standard for voir dire is to create a comfortable courtroom atmosphere where jurors feel safe disclosing *honest* answers. It is only by effectively collecting and interpreting honest information shared by potential jurors that lawyers can intelligently exercise peremptory challenges and challenges for cause. A voir dire process without open and honest jurors is deeply flawed because it taints the many decisions that flow from their answers, particularly the all-important decisions to strike or keep jurors.

We provide the venire a comfortable environment producing honest answers by viewing and treating jurors as aces to ensure they *feel* like aces in court. As a non-exhaustive list, we mention a few things lawyers can do to create the proper environment. To draw upon one of our four rules, a simple "Yes and" mentality gets a lawyer on the right track. The "Yes and..." attitude creates trust because it validates the jurors' ideas, rather than halting progress by destroying their ideas. Looping a juror's answer, for instance, acknowledges you listened to the answer and to some extent lends credence to their answer. Incidentally, a juror's opinion that is contrary or in some way at odds with your case theory might be a reason to strike that juror, yet it in no way makes the opinion wrong.

Lawyers also need to pay attention, listen and be polite, starting with common courtesies such as a simple "please" or "thank you." At times lawyers lose their sense of humanity in court, perhaps by stiffly addressing the venire in a way that creates a figurative wall between lawyer and jurors. "Where are you employed?", or "Do you promise you will hold my opponents to their burden...?" Incidentally, the language selected as much as the tone contributes to creating the wall. Why not ask politely, "Where do you work...," "Would you mind sharing...," or "I know this is a difficult topic, but..."

In social settings outside the courtroom, when friends or acquaintances reveal they or someone close to them have had a devastating experience or illness, human beings naturally acknowledge the experience empathetically by saying, "I'm so sorry to hear that," or "I'm so sorry that happened and you are going through that." Yet how often do we see a scene like this during voir dire:

> Lawyer: "Have any jurors had any problems with drunk drivers" (One hand goes up) "Yes, Ms. Jones?"
>
> Ms. Jones: "A drunk driver ran over and killed my husband and three kids."
>
> Lawyer: (without hesitating and perhaps "attending" to a pen and notes) "Ok. Anyone else?"

Not listening empathetically to jurors is greatly problematic, but losing all sense of humanity is inexcusable. An appropriate response, not that there is only one, would be, "I'm very sorry you went through that experience, I know it is difficult to talk about. Thank you for sharing."

A lawyer's self-disclosure by sharing a brief personal story during voir dire tends to increase comfort level and help elicit honest and open answers from the venire. Just as people tend to "mirror" others' behavior, the idea that "I'll show you mine if you show me yours...," applies to voir dire. A lawyer's anecdote creates a comfort level for jurors to open up. After self-disclosure, the lawyer should then of course listen empathetically to potential jurors, rather than talking and waiting to talk.

Lawyers must also understand that they cannot change a juror's values or opinions during voir dire. Assuming a juror indicates she cannot "presume someone is innocent," essentially revealing that she believes the accused did something wrong simply because he is charged, the lawyer cannot change those feelings. Lawyers might commonly ask, "Would you presume Mr. Smith innocent if the judge instructed you *must* do so...?" However, this question during a few minutes of voir dire, even if answered affirmatively, generally cannot and will not change long held beliefs.

A good benchmark for a productive and successful voir dire is that prospective jurors speak ninety percent of the time while the lawyers speak ten percent of the time. With this ninety percent/ten percent rule allowing jurors to reveal more information, lawyers all but guarantee they have more ammunition to make intelligent decisions about challenges. More importantly, the jurors can rightfully claim their status as aces.

With few exceptions, voir dire is the only time during trial that jurors speak at length, much less at all. For the rest of the show, they take notes, remain quiet, watch, and, hopefully, listen, until they get back to the jury room to deliberate and run the show. At every chance during voir dire, we should let the jurors know that they are aces.

DELIBERATIONS: WHO IS IN CHARGE NOW?

After recognizing the importance of elevating the jurors' status, particularly during voir dire, their appropriate and desired status crystallizes when they receive jury instructions, exhibits and other demonstrative evidence to deliberate. We cede all power to them and pass the baton as they begin processing and deciding, favorably or unfavorably, our client's fate. The jurors now press all the buttons, pull all the strings and take charge.

The lawyer sits and prays if religious, and if not, thinks some pleasant thoughts because with the exception of some limited, minimal and at best indirect input, perhaps as the judge answers questions submitted by jurors during deliberations, the lawyer holds no more influence. With our status significantly diminished, we can only hope to have done everything possible to send the proper signals while the opportunity presented itself. Just as status changes frequently, much like the judge who goes home to her teenage daughter, the status relationship between jurors and lawyers changes considerably at the inception of the deliberation.

We now consider the effect of status pertaining to the relationships *among* jurors. When jurors deliberate they undoubtedly enter a unique world with some formal rules, yet really no rules at all. Before deliberations the judge theoretically "instructed" jurors with a long, boring and legalistic list of instructions. These so-called "pattern" instructions on the law usually provide little or no guidance about the deliberation procedures, *how* they should deliberate or *what* they should talk about. Jurors might pay little if any attention to jury instructions.

Thrown into a jury room like school children released onto the playground, they begin a process that is one step away from chaos. Children released onto the playground without parental guidance begin to socialize, create factions or cliques, and develop their own rules. During this process they establish a hierarchy based on status. Whether defined by size, gender, athletic ability or intelligence, the children separate and then create relationships to find out where they fit into the hierarchy.

Although the status hierarchy process for jurors possibly started long before deliberations during the voir dire and evidentiary phases of the trial, jurors face much of the same situation as children when they begin deliberating. The jurors, too, will create a hierarchy based on status. After focusing on the individual job of listening to the evidence, they must now *collectively* decide the case during this critical and new deliberation phase.

To start deliberations, the group takes little to nothing from the judge's insufficient, legalistic and likely incomprehensive instructions, perhaps with the exception that they must elect a foreperson. Interestingly, one of the first things a jury does, as instructed, is elevate the status of the one person they elect or choose as foreperson. The foreperson serves as a pillar of sorts during deliberations and will most often significantly impact the deliberation process. Predicting a foreperson is a guess at best and often impossible, yet attorneys are justifiably and legitimately concerned about who was selected to the exclusion of all others as the "go to" person and leader of the deliberation. One of the finest jury selectors, the legendary Cathy "Cat" Bennett, did in fact predict the foreperson in Roy Black's successful defense of William Kennedy Smith.

With a limited number of challenges and some otherwise similarly situated jurors, a lawyer should consider during voir dire which prospective juror, based on personality, attitudes or position in employment, might serve as the foreperson and have an increased impact on the deliberation. Typically, the voir dire process is never perfect. Likewise, we seldom if ever select twelve jurors who are perfect to hear and accept the story you present. But deliberations in particular, guided by a juror with a high status and strong personality, who in some regards is unfavorable to your case, can be significantly detrimental.

Lawyers might also prognosticate somewhat about which jurors will likely play a minimal, if any, role in the deliberations. These issues rightfully pique a lawyer's interest because the entire jury process will be permeated by status. A good trial lawyer does not dwell on this issue but certainly recognizes its importance by keeping it on the radar to gain an edge wherever possible.

ADVOCACY DEFINED AND GUIDED BY STATUS

We also consider how status affects case preparation and presentation from the jurors' viewpoints. Pre-trial preparation of the client's story and case theory includes facts, characters, scenes, emotions and to some extent the law. Because we elevate jurors to aces in the hierarchical chain, we do everything to mold, prepare and present our story with the jurors in mind.

We might develop strong emotions and animosity, for instance, during pre-trial litigation based on adversarial situations with opposing counsel. Or maybe we had unfriendly and at times downright hostile confrontations with opposing witnesses during hearings or depositions. We must however put these experiences aside and focus solely on the jury.

The jury is unaware of this back-story and we need to consciously ignore personal grudges and let the jurors' sensibilities guide every decision we make in the court. We use emotion to prepare and present our story but those emotions derive solely from our client's story and the jurors' needs.

We break down the story characters to fit them most advantageously into our theory according to our status hierarchy. What status will an unbiased eyewitness or expert have in the jurors' eyes? Is the witness a complaining witness or a true victim, and what, if any, effect will this distinction have on status? Given a witness' status and the vast array of emotions, attitude and demeanor available to us, how should we treat the witness in court? Most importantly, do we want to diminish or elevate a witness' status in the eyes of jurors, and if so, how can we do that?

We should brainstorm and answer these and other related questions while preparing the case, and certainly before voir dire.

WHERE DOES MY CLIENT STAND?
WHERE *SHOULD* MY CLIENT STAND?

We also consider where our client falls in the status hierarchy in the jurors' eyes. Generally, a client who attains high status in their eyes will hopefully achieve a successful outcome. In some instances, jurors might not hold anyone in high status. Rather, they decide a case by choosing the lesser of two evils.

With some clients we have little work to do to get them into a position of high status in the jurors' eyes. Keep in mind that while jurors might put a sympathetic, likeable client on a high pedestal in the courtroom, that position does not necessarily equate with high status. A less sympathetic and less likable client such as an accused killer or perhaps an insurance company presents a greater hurdle. Many jurors will initially relegate them to low status.

Regardless of the client, we generally endeavor to raise their status because jurors might defer to clients with elevated status. Jurors might not view our accused killer as an ace, but elevating his status, to any extent possible, will inevitably help our cause.

These status considerations are fluid and nuanced based on our client and case theory. We might, for instance, face hurdles with a client with high status at a sentencing hearing. A sentencing judge looking at the high status of a convicted politician might say, "He should have known better!" On the other hand, a low status client at sentencing might be an easier sell for a lower sentence – "I'm sorry. I made a mistake and did not mean to do it."

HOW TO ELEVATE YOUR CLIENT'S STATUS (BEFORE, DURING AND AFTER OPENING STATEMENT)

In the eyes of the jurors, how can we elevate our client's status perhaps while simultaneously diminishing, if necessary, the status of our opponents' witnesses and/or client? These two endeavors often go hand-in-hand, as the act of raising our client's status will sometimes necessarily diminish, as a byproduct, the status of our opponent's client and/or witnesses.

We can tilt the status pendulum in our favor by demonstrating a genuine commitment to our client's cause in several ways. Everything from language to body language, as well as little things we do in the courtroom, can affect our client's success.

First off, we should always refer to a client by name. Although it sounds simple and it is simple, many lawyers habitually refer to clients as "my client." Whether getting a simple continuance or trying a case, lawyers should habitually and instinctively refer to clients by name. Clients deserve this. Humanizing a client can be a great hurdle in many cases and the process starts long before the trial.

By its very nature the word "client" creates distance between you and "James Murphy," for instance. It connotes a business relationship that is somehow forced and unnatural, whether due to money or judicial appointment. At best it implies a distant relationship between lawyer and client, and at worst it implies a lawyer's lack of commitment.

The word "client," in fact, not only connotes a business and professional relationship, but by its very *meaning* literally *designates a difference in status*. The word "client" originated in ancient Rome to describe a plebeian who was dependent on a patrician patron. (See also the Latin word "cliens," which means "follower.") This original meaning specifically and in no uncertain terms designated a "client" as a person of *lower status*. The term is inconsistent with and contrary to our goal of elevating our client's status because it has the inherent net effect of lowering our client's status. Of course we use the word "client" generically throughout this book, but our purpose in court differs significantly.

Using our client's name begins the often difficult process of humanizing them by demonstrating our commitment to their case to everyone in the courtroom. Even when dealing with judges before trial, it positively affects our purpose by demonstrating the uniqueness of the case to clearly signal it is not simply "another" case on a long docket of cases.

Because the opportunities of elevating a client's status before opening statement are in most instances limited, opening statement often offers the best chance to do so. We must seize the inherent drama of the opening as the first chance to tell a client's story and allow jurors to see our client through different eyes according to our theory. We demonstrate commitment to the case by telling a powerful opening story where at a minimum we humanize our client and emotionally connect him to the jurors, using effective tone, expression and body language. These things give jurors reason to elevate a client's status.

Undoubtedly jurors construct their own story as they hear and see evidence. Before they do so, however, we elevate our client's status through a persuasive opening story that provides an unwavering theory and solid framework for their story. Winning at trial usually results when jurors fill in *their* story according to *our* theory.

After opening statement, each cross-examination and/ or impeachment of our opponents' witnesses diminishes their credibility and simultaneously diminishes their status. Hopefully, as a reciprocal effect, the jurors will simultaneously, if incrementally, raise our client's and our witnesses' status.

We later discuss space in the courtroom. For now we note spatial concepts to elevate the status of a testifying client or witness. Rather than standing in front of the jury box while a client or witness testifies, we stand with the jury box between you and the witness box. In this way, you remove yourself physically from the jurors' sight line so their attention focuses on the witness. Hopefully, their testimony *to* the jurors will demonstrate that our client honors their status.

STATUS IN STORYTELLING

Looking directly at our client's story, we also give due consideration to status and how it affected the story. What were the positions of the parties involved? Did the police officer's status affect the story? If so, how? What other status relationships affected the story and how? Did the status of the characters change, and if so, what effect did the changes have on the story? Thus, we apply our understanding of status to our client's story to best understand how to present the story at trial.

The effect of status in the courtroom can be fruitfully explored and discussed further. Improv merely opens the door to our awareness of status as an omnipresent part of communication and a phenomenon that permeates brainstorming and case presentation.

V.

EMOTIONAL RANGE

"I've learned that people will forget what you said,
people will forget what you did, but people will
never forget how you made them feel."

— Maya Angelou

"Conductor: 'When you play that phrase
it should sound like the heavens opening,
like all of humanity crying out with joy.'
Trombones: 'So do you want it louder or softer?'"

— Unknown

"Words mean more than what is
set down on paper. It takes the human voice
to infuse them with deeper meaning."

— Maya Angelou

"Tain't what you do it's the way that you do it
and that's what gets results."

— Ella Fitzgerald

INTRODUCTION

Emotions are significant to trial work for two reasons, which inevitably become intertwined. First, we develop and use emotions in court to *present* a case to jurors. Because a monotonous voice devoid of expression and *emotion* will surely put jurors to sleep, we develop emotional range of expression and practice those skills before we get to the courtroom. Our goal is not to make actors out of lawyers but simply to draw on the actors' craft to make lawyers more powerful communicators. How will a lawyer use emotion when trying a case? Are the emotions used productive or counterproductive? Are nerves, or "butterflies" an issue, and if so, how can we get the butterflies to fly in formation?

We started to explore the second area when using the "Advance, Color, Emotion" exercise. Specifically, we noted that lawyers need to recognize the specific, fluid and ever-changing emotional states of characters in order to most powerfully and persuasively tell a story in court. What specific emotions motivate characters? How do those emotions change as the story progresses? What emotions drive the important scenes and the story as a whole? How can we best use the mélange of emotions inherent in a case to benefit a client?

We will discuss the above two topics and use improv exercises to develop emotional range skills for the courtroom.

EMOTIONAL RANGE IN PRESENTING OUR CASE

Lawyers too seldom take time to recognize the emotions available to them while on trial. They even more infrequently explore emotional range and actually *practice* those skills. With a law school background emphasizing logic rather than emotion, they often find it unnecessary and indeed scary to move out of their comfort zone to work on emotional range. Through improv, we explore emotions and learn how to effectively express both simple and complex emotions.

People commonly and naturally feel and experience a wide variety of basic and complex emotions. Expressing those emotions is another matter, particularly when we try to reproduce those emotions in court. Emotions in court are often uncomfortable or ineffective, and at times they feel unusual or inappropriate.

Lawyers often limit themselves in court to basic emotions and, unfortunately, one of the most widely used courtroom emotions is self-righteous indignation or some variation of anger. Unaccustomed to expressing a good variety of emotions, we seldom consider in court how to best convey an effective variety of emotions.

In our daily lives, we perhaps only occasionally express complex emotions, yet the courtroom requires us to explore, recognize and have great fluency expressing those emotions. Some emotions are unfamiliar to us because we have not experienced them, yet in court we must tell stories that integrally engage and elicit many unfamiliar emotions. "The truth is stranger than fiction," as they say, and real life stories are complex, involved, and often far beyond our personal experiences, both factually and emotionally.

Effective lawyering demands investing in and committing to a client's cause by fully exploring, recognizing and understanding the entire emotional range of a story, including unfamiliar emotions. Maybe we have not walked into a bedroom to find a cheating spouse in coitus and experienced the jealous rage that precedes a homicide. Nor have we felt the overwhelming fear for our own life that precedes a killing in self-defense.

Yet lawyers need to walk in those shoes by taking more than a casual, factual and detached stroll through those events. In preparing for trial we need to saunter, gallop and run in those shoes by diving headfirst into those scenes, exploring the story from every angle and immersing fervently in the case until we fully understand the emotions in the story. Every trial demands and deserves this level of preparation. Indeed, after a thorough emotional assessment of a story, jurors will *feel* that you've been there.

Expanding emotional range by exploring and learning to express emotions also makes us better, more persuasive communicators because we recognize and understand that what appears to be a single emotion can and will often vary in degree along a continuum, existing to a lesser or greater extent. Take, for example, happiness. A baseball fan feels happy when their team wins a preseason game, which is happiness on the lower level of the continuum. The level of happiness increases when the same fan watches their team win a regular season game, and increases even more when the team wins a playoff game. In each example, the fan is happy, but in varying and increasing degrees.

We recognize further that these are different and distinct, albeit similar, emotions within emotional range. The same baseball fan, upon seeing their team win the

World Series, will be happy on perhaps the highest level of the continuum of happiness. That fan is now perhaps *elated*, as the happiness morphs into differing degrees, and likewise into a different emotion, in this case-elation. Thus, we recognize not only the varying degrees of emotions within a story but also different and distinct emotions. Most characters usually feel a variety of emotions and at times, the same emotion on different levels of a continuum.

Might we develop an emotional range that is in excess of what we actually need or use in the courtroom? The short answer is 'yes,' and we use a basketball analogy to explain.

Basketball players will not, except in dire circumstances and having no other choice, shoot from the half-court line in a game. In practice, however, players develop and increase shooting range to gain an understanding of the *limits* of their range. In basketball, every player must know the maximum distance from which they can shoot accurately and effectively. Thus, in a practice setting, usually after practice, a player will launch the ball up to the rim from increasing distances in an effort to find their true range.

Missed shots from afar, if nothing else, give the shooter more confidence in taking more appropriate shots. Indeed, the closer shots become easier. The shooter inevitably makes a few long-distance shots from beyond the appropriate range, all the while developing muscles and gaining comfort level. In the event the player has no choice but to take that shot in a game, they will have more confidence taking those shots.

Lawyers most likely will not express excessive emotions in court by going over the top, as it might not best serve their story, their own credibility, and of course, their client. However, the practice outside of court, of going over the top in exploring and *expressing* emotions stretches the lawyer's emotional range. The process also makes it more comfortable to access *appropriate* courtroom emotion by enhancing and empowering the lawyer's emotional range skills. When a case requires a lawyer to delve into the uncomfortable terrain of expressing unusual, unfamiliar or excessive emotions, the jump will be a comfortable one the lawyer can make with confidence, knowing they have *actually been there* before.

The lawyer's role and credibility differ from that of an actor as we do not pretend to be someone we are not, yet we should prepare for trial by going over the top to accurately explore and understand emotions to the same extent as our characters. We will better empathize with those characters, even if the process comes at the risk of looking foolish during our pre-trial preparation, and we will tell our client's story more persuasively and powerfully to jurors.

How then can we develop the ability to recognize, distinguish and express different emotions? Also, when our story calls for it, how can we develop the ability to shift gears?

OPPOSITE EMOTIONS AND EVERYTHING IN BETWEEN

Let's first consider and develop emotional range by exploring how we can take two contrasting emotions, on opposite ends of a spectrum, to create a continuum of differing expression. To explore the continuum of emotions, we will use an exercise we will call "nasty to nice," as we explore differing expressions based upon these two emotions. Imagine for a minute a scale of one to ten upon which we are going to create a continuum of our two emotions: nice and nasty.

1	2	3	4	5	6	7	8	9	10
Nice				Matter of Fact					Nasty

The five represents a normal tone of voice that is rather matter of fact. As we move from the five toward the one, we are getting increasingly nice, to the point where, at the one, we are speaking in a tone of voice as if speaking to our beloved, dying, saintly grandmother, who is on her deathbed. Our expression, as we talk to our grandmother, will be as nice as we can possibly talk to anyone.

As we move from the one to the five, our expression becomes increasingly, and in roughly equal increments, more matter of fact. Continuing on from our five, matter of fact position to the right, we will move incrementally and increasingly toward our nasty side. When we get to ten, we are emotionally at the nastiest point we can be, as if we are speaking to the person who has just pilfered all our money, burned down our house and stolen our first born.

Moving *randomly* among the numbers on the scale, we practice a presentation, perhaps an opening statement or closing argument. As the number changes, the lawyer commits to portraying as accurately as possible the emotion associated with that number. While the extremes on the scale, particularly when done in succession (i.e. moving from 1 to 10), obviously produce the greatest discrepancy and most entertainment, it is also important for lawyers to navigate and emote accurately the nuances of the numbers in between, so as to fine tune their ability to emote with increasing precision.

Before discussing this exercise further, let's make something clear. When a lawyer properly does this exercise by accurately committing to each emotion it will be clear that the ten, nine, eight and possibly seven will seldom if ever be used in a courtroom. The increasingly nasty attitude in numbers seven through ten, in most instances, is seldom if ever justified and almost always inappropriate in court as it will turn off jurors.

However, practicing those areas of the scale does a couple of things for lawyers. Some lawyers easily succumb to the temptation to get confrontational, or worse yet angry, at the earliest invitation. They view themselves as warriors and mistakenly feel that anger and raised voices are effective.

Perhaps anger can sometimes genuinely and productively express a willingness to posture and fight for a client or highlight an injustice. However, it is most often used as an attempt to establish a status that is unnecessary and counterproductive. It is simply an ineffective reaction to something that occurred. Outwardly expressing anger while *practicing* a presentation will demonstrate the ineffectiveness of the 7–10 range.

We will often however productively use the one through six range in court. Particularly on cross-examination, we need to consider our demeanor and how we treat witnesses. As a rule we should not be cross while we do cross. While impeaching a witness with an inconsistent statement, for instance, we might say, "You never told the police the car was blue," in two distinct ways. First, near a one on the scale, we tacitly say, "I understand, we all make mistakes," and then perhaps a bit higher on the scale, we let the jurors *feel* that this witness is lying.

MIRRORING

Let's digress briefly to discuss mirroring, as it relates to the idea that you do not have to be cross to do cross. Mirroring as a phenomenon occurs every day in ordinary communication and it certainly is no stranger to the courtroom. Mirroring occurs when one party to a conversation communicates in a certain way and the person or people on the receiving end of the conversation then subconsciously act similarly by imitating or mirroring the first person's emotions, attitude and even body language. This mirroring can create rapport.

For example, friends might converse initially in a low, somber tone. However, when one party to the conversation reacts in a different tone, perhaps excitedly and with increased volume, others in the conversation tend to respond in kind and follow suit. Or, for instance, a group of people converse loudly and excitedly, when suddenly one participant speaks at a near whisper, bringing a slower, softer tone to the conversation. This change likewise causes the group to follow suit.

Mirroring also applies to the courtroom. Specifically, when a cross examiner outwardly emotes an attack mode, a witness often responds similarly. Thus, lawyers should avoid succumbing to the tempting pitfall of jumping into the six-plus range during cross examination, instead staying in the more productive and effective 1–5 range. The witness will often mirror the examiner. Incidentally, during opening statement or closing argument, a nodding head used in conjunction with a rhetorical question will often cause the juror on the other end to nod back.

Juxtaposing the high and low ends of the above scale demonstrates to lawyers the overall ineffectiveness of operating in the higher ends. Lawyers can then work toward sharpening and refining the 1–5 range skills. This concept of using opposite emotions on a 1–10 scale continuum works effectively with other emotions as well to increase emotional range.

To fine tune speaking skills, we also use a 1–10 scale for speed or volume, as discussed above. By doing so we learn to comfortably use different volumes and speeds, most notably the *lower* volumes and *slower* speeds which are effective but often ignored in court. Intertwining different volumes and pacing also bolsters our emotional range.

THE DEVELOPMENT OF A VARIETY OF SPECIFIC AND COMPLEX EMOTIONS

After exploring opposite emotions on a continuum, we explore the effective expression of a variety of specific emotions. Like the "nasty to nice" scale, our exploration of specific, unique emotions expands emotional range skills in the courtroom. To do so, lawyers must be willing to step outside the serious context of court and act a bit silly.

We emphasize one of our four rules. Specifically, the lawyer must invest in this exercise with reckless abandon and without fear of making mistakes or looking silly. Though many lawyers do this exercise reluctantly, they inevitably find they have and can develop far more emotional range than ever imagined.

First we choose an easily memorized song or poem, often times a children's song. For instance, you can use the "Happy Birthday" song, the "Itsy Bitsy Spider," or any other song that is short but easily memorized. The lawyer then focuses on expressing different emotions while reciting the song.

To make this exercise successful, the lawyer must commit to the specific emotion and go over the top with that feeling by outwardly expressing the emotion precisely. We repeat the song, each time expressing and portraying a different, specific emotion. The list of emotions is limitless but we focus initially on basic emotions such as happiness, sadness, anger, or indifference. Then we do the same exercise with more complex emotions such as confusion, optimism, pessimism, paranoia and envy.

When performed properly, a listener easily determines with certainty the specific sentiment expressed because the lawyer successfully emotes effectively and precisely. The lawyer begins to *internalize* the ability to accurately portray emotions. After the lawyer accurately portrays basic emotions and the listener easily receives the intended message, the lawyer then explores more complex emotions.

This exercise enables lawyers to gain comfort expressing both simple and complex emotions. Once accomplished and lawyers start to develop and explore emotional range, we use improv to work with emotions in greater depth by creating a skit in a group setting using an imaginary park bench.

Guided by our four rules, the exercise starts with two strangers sitting on a park bench. Each person portrays an emotion provided by a director on a small piece of paper. We will refer to them as "lawyer one" and "lawyer two." Their own emotion is unbeknownst to the other person on the bench as well as the group that watches the conversation. While improvising dialogue and creating a skit, they focus on accurately demonstrating and portraying their particular emotion by using every fiber of their being, including body language, expression and dialogue, without of course making any specific reference to that emotion such as, "I'm so paranoid of everything."

The scene continues for a few minutes followed by the director sending "lawyer three" to the park bench with a new emotion, also written on a piece of paper and unknown to anyone else in the group. Upon seeing lawyer three approaching, lawyer one improvises some reason for leaving the park bench and exiting the scene. Lawyers two and three then engage in a skit while maintaining their commitment to their respective emotions. The skit continues until everyone has a chance to sit and interact on the bench.

When the exercise ends, the group as a whole will guess what specific emotions each lawyer portrayed. The challenge is to portray each emotion so precisely that it will be differentiated from similar but distinct emotions. Can the group distinguish envy from jealousy, or optimism from happiness? When done well, the group will specifically pinpoint each emotion, and incidentally, create many laughs.

People who might not otherwise think of themselves as funny will inevitably be funny through improvised dialogue due to the collision of different emotions and the willingness to commit to their respective emotions. This alone is worth the price of admission as lawyers gain self-confidence. It also allows lawyers the opportunity to experience first-hand and jump head first into a variety of complex emotions including but certainly not limited to paranoid, jealous, optimistic and cynical. More than simply expressing an emotion, as in the "birthday song" exercise, they now use every fiber of their being to *portray* an emotion.

Once lawyers can recognize emotions and express them to the extent that the feeling is immediately apparent to a *listener,* the lawyer has developed significant and invaluable emotional range skills for the courtroom.

EMOTIONS OF THE CHARACTERS AND STORY AT TRIAL

In addition to acquiring the ability to express emotions in a way that connects with a listener, we also prepare for trial by exploring the emotions inherent in our client's story. After all, the ability to express emotion accurately is only valuable to a trial lawyer if and when those skills make the story at trial more plausible and compelling. Thus, we explore, recognize and decipher the emotions at play in a client's story to use emotional range skills in a manner supportive of our case theory. Guided by our theory, we break down the characters of the story to decide what emotions are most critical to our story as a whole. We of course explore the entire story from an emotional standpoint, including our opponent's characters/witnesses, as we endeavor to get jurors emotionally hooked and committed to *our* side of the case.

A case is most often in court because something bad happened. Referring back to our "Once upon a time" formula, we recall that something in the tilt ("But one day/ because of that") part of the formula detrimentally impacted someone's life. Most characters' emotional states change regularly. Most notably, the tilt will typically ignite a significant emotional change. Our exploration and understanding of the changing emotions of all the characters, together with our ability to accurately and effectively express emotional range, allow us to present characters accurately and tell the story most persuasively.

Looking again at the drug case of William Smith, we see a case that is not, at least on face level, bubbling with emotion. Our challenge is to explore his story on an emotional level and extract emotions from the story that allow us to connect emotionally with jurors, with the goal of getting William acquitted.

Starting the process by using the "Once upon a time" formula, we uncovered some of the emotions of the characters that will help us connect with jurors on an emotional level. With the backbone of the story intact, we apply the "Advance-Color-Emotion" technique, only this time we apply the emotional element in a manner that is choreographed with and supportive of our theory. Considering William's changing emotional state, we brainstorm the emotions that motivated him throughout the ordeal. We will use those feelings to connect with jurors and make them comfortable acquitting him.

Initially, he is a happy-go-lucky, ordinary young man looking for some healthy recreation after a school day. He is relaxed, comfortable and carefree during the

"Everyday...," part of the story as he heads to the park. His emotional state changes, however, as he sees the police approach. Although he knows he has done nothing wrong, he feels that he is hanging around some less than stellar characters likely to attract trouble. His emotional state then becomes curious or wary as he wonders why the police are approaching.

As they walk toward him, he becomes anxious and nervous and when handcuffed, as an innocent man who has had his freedom restricted, he is deeply disappointed, knowing he has done nothing wrong. That disappointment turns to anger when he realizes that his life, inexplicably, has turned upside down for no reason. He might later experience regret for hanging out with the wrong people, fear for not knowing what will become of the situation, and eventually, righteous indignation knowing he is innocent.

After exploring and recognizing these different and changing emotions we draw upon these emotions to tell William's story in court, noting that perhaps the best chance of acquittal is to get the jurors to understand and empathize with him emotionally. Noting that all three prongs of Aristotle's theory of persuasion-ethos (credibility of the speaker), logos (logic or reason), and pathos (appeal to emotion) - undoubtedly have their rightful place in the courtroom, we focus here on emotional appeal, and more specifically, how we can get the jurors to *connect emotionally* with William.

To use pathos to convince jurors we ask several questions. Which emotions do we want the jury to focus on? Which emotions allow the jurors to best walk in his shoes? Which emotions if understood and accepted will make the jurors sympathize with him? These are some of the questions we brainstorm to prepare to tell his story.

We also explore the prosecution case on an emotional level to incorporate those emotions, when appropriate, into our story. Perhaps we have young, anxious police officers with adrenaline flowing. They are excited and pumped-up about making the arrest.

We digress for a moment to note an example of how emotions can be complex. Earlier we noted William's anxiety as the police officers approached. His anxiety, however, is distinguishable from the officer's anxiety. William's anxiety stems from a gut feeling and ominous sign that something bad is about to happen, while the officer's anxiety stems from excitement and the hope something good is about to happen. In using emotional range to express anxiety, we recognize the distinguishable and significant difference between the two types of anxiety. We must express the emotion accurately to send the right signal to jurors, so they feel and understand exactly what we intend.

Returning to the officers' emotions, their anxiety and excitement turns to a businesslike attitude as they move in to make an arrest. Perhaps a no-holds-barred attitude dominates as they actually make the arrest, followed by satisfaction and gloating once William is handcuffed.

After we understand all the characters' emotions and how those emotions played into their actions, we then look back at the story on a macroscopic level. How can we use emotion to connect with jurors? How can we persuade jurors on an emotional level and get them to side with William? To do so, we collect the most powerful, overriding emotions of the case and integrate them into our story. We, of course, keep close at hand the status elements of the characters, recognizing that similar to emotions, a theory based recognition and application of status also makes the story more persuasive.

At times, the fluctuating emotions of a story actually drive our theory. For example, when someone robs a woman of her purse on the street, we recognize the changing emotions of the victim to defend the person accused of the robbery. The woman initially walks home from work *inattentively* as she thinks about work, dinner and seeing her family. When confronted from behind by a threatening stranger holding an object that appears to be a weapon, she becomes *frightened*. Alas, she goes to the police department, now feeling safe but full of *vengefulness*. In defending the case, these three emotions inform how we connect the jurors emotionally to our theory.

While walking inattentively, the victim did not *pay attention* to the perpetrator. Because she was frightened by the robber she *did not get a good look at him*, perhaps succumbing to "gun focus," and her overriding need for justice and vengefulness explains why she *picked an innocent man out of a lineup*. Creating this emotional connection between our story and the jurors will help us win the gold medal at trial.

APPROPRIATE USE OF EMOTIONAL RANGE IN THE COURTROOM

Though we use an effective emotional range arsenal, we must consider both its limits and appropriate use in court. Through our basketball analogy we noted the need and reason for developing an emotional range that admittedly exceeds what we actually use in court.

Incidentally, experience suggests that lawyers who go over the top are the exception. More often, lawyers express themselves without enough emotion, some even speaking in a monotone voice that likely puts jurors to sleep. In any event, it is easier to scale back and decrease emotional range in a courtroom performance than it is to get lawyers to use sufficient, appropriate emotion.

We know that *how* something is said, usually more so than *what* is said, makes a world of difference. The same statement spoken with different tones and attitudes conveys a distinctly different idea and feeling. Lawyers can and should use a powerful, well-developed emotional range to persuade. However, appropriate emotional range in court should be tempered, subtle and nuanced. Assume the focus of an inconsistent statement impeachment is the color of car. All facts are not equal, and for our purpose we use proper emphasis. "When you gave your truthful, accurate and complete statement to the police, you said the car was *red*," with emphasis and proper inflection on red.

As actors portray a character's emotions, they often emote far more excessively than what is appropriate in court. Actors must *convince* an audience of the authenticity of their character. To do so, they accurately commit to the character's emotions as a necessary part of creating a compelling, believable character. If portraying the character calls for an actor to emote in an excessive or over the top manner, the actor does so to accurately portray the character's genuine emotions.

Lawyers are not actors. Lawyers in court have credibility

expectations that differ vastly from actors portraying characters. The actor convinces an audience they are a different person, while a trial lawyer simply advocates on behalf of the client whose story is entrusted to them. If lawyers go over the top to the same extent as actors, jurors might likely find it somewhat amusing or entertaining but not necessarily credible. An acting performance in court, especially going far over the top, runs the strong risk of becoming a stunt or gimmick in the jurors' eyes. Worse yet, jurors might view it as an effort to distract them from the true story because the lawyer's performance does not comport with jurors' expectations.

Thus, a lawyer should focus on exploring and recognizing emotions intrinsic to a client's story, developing effective skills to express a significant array of emotions and using those skills in a nuanced and appropriate way to persuasively tell the client's story in court.

EMOTIONS OF THE LAWYER AND NERVES

How do a lawyer's emotions play into courtroom performance and, where necessary, how can we control those emotions? While effectively expressing emotion to tell a story in court, we must also control the extent to which we let our involvement in a case dictate our own emotions at trial.

To some extent, we must temper *our* emotional involvement in the story so it does not interfere with our persuasive abilities. Lawyers must keep their emotions in check and always retain the ability to access their entire emotional range, as appropriate, rather than being driven by dominant, overriding emotions.

We need to consider a lawyer's emotions in terms of the jurors' sensibilities. A lawyer's emotions at trial are at times driven by the backstory, not only of the client's story, but also of the procedural development of the case. Oftentimes before trial, counsel has a lengthy involvement in the case. They develop biases and motivations based upon adverse, and at times, confrontational relationships with others involved in the case, including opposing counsels and witnesses.

On some level this backstory motivates the lawyer, yet the jurors are obviously and entirely unfamiliar with this backstory. Thus, to the extent a lawyer reacts emotionally in court as a result of this backstory, the jurors are at best confused. They perhaps read the lawyer as acting inappropriately because they don't have the same basis of knowledge. This of course works to the client's disadvantage because jurors hold the lawyer's behavior, and what they see as inappropriate emotion, against the client throughout the case and possibly into the deliberation room.

For instance, a lawyer and witness have a hostile relationship because they sparred during a pre-trial hearing. At trial, the lawyer impeaches the witness in an inappropriate, uncivilized and overly confrontational manner. Though the lawyer might feel this emotional reaction was appropriate in front of the jury, the jury undoubtedly views the lawyer as an overbearing bully and the lawyer loses credibility in their eyes. The lawyer's emotional reaction is neither understandable nor acceptable to them and unfortunately, the client suffers. This is a detrimental display of emotion.

The elephant in the living room of emotions that perhaps nags lawyers more so than most others is stage-fright. Some studies suggest many people's greatest fear is public speaking, followed by snakes and death. If true, people would rather die or suffer a snake bite than speak in public. Many lawyers feel some form of this emotion. For some, it is extreme stage-fright with physical symptoms. Others have a milder case of "butterflies" or "nerves." This nervous state results in large part from the fear of being judged.

For purposes of courtroom performance, we consider the prevalence of this emotion, whether it affects us detrimentally and if so, what we can do to rectify the problem.

For good reason, some people believe that if you do not experience some form of "nerves" on trial, it is time to get out of the business. According to this sentiment, our nerves surface because we actually *care* about what we do and the absence of nerves signals the time to move on to a new career. While this perhaps is partially true, this theory does not acknowledge that two situations, a lack of nerves and trying a case, might not be mutually exclusive.

Indeed, some people simply do not get nervous when trying cases and others channel potentially hazardous nerves into positive, productive courtroom presentations. Our concern is the many lawyers who do experience nerves with some real or perceived adverse effects, and how they can effectively control and use those nerves.

Like most of life's endeavors, practice makes perfect and there is no substitute for experience, especially live practices for trials or appellate arguments in front of other people. Experience trying cases inevitably helps deal with problematic nerves, and practicing opening statements or closing arguments inevitably makes the real show go down a whole lot smoother. Experienced or not, there is no substitute for *preparation.* Extensive and thorough preparation through which you get a solid handle on your presentation eliminates one of the greatest causes of the fear of speaking – not being ready to "perform."

Indeed, extensive preparation makes an otherwise shaky performance a *confident* performance. Besides preparation, practice and experience, we deal with nerves by allowing our body to relax, which of course is easier said than done. To relax in front of jurors, we abide by the old adage that we concentrate on *what* we are doing, not *how* we are doing. For some lawyers, using mantras or rituals will help.

Throughout the spectrum of improv exercises, we develop the ability to ignore our inner critic. As problematic nerves interfere during courtroom performance, to a great degree, our mind, and more specifically our inner critic, constantly criticizes by casting doubt and telling us we are doing something wrong. Improv prepares and trains us to ignore the inner critic in court. We learn to prevent "it" from invading our thought process and we rid ourselves of destructive nerves and fear. Most importantly, we will perform confidently in court by constantly focusing on *what* we are doing, not *how* we are doing.

Nerves can also disrupt us in court by causing our minds to race along at a breakneck pace, functioning at speeds that far exceed our verbal abilities. Many lawyers habitually speak too quickly while their mind races along and attempts to drag their speech along with it. Most lawyers will solve this problem by simply speaking *slowly*.

For the many lawyers that speak too quickly, we practice an opening statement before trial by speaking *uuunnnnuuuuusssuuaaallly slooooowly,* to break this cycle. In court, we can consciously establish a slow, controlled speech pattern, particularly during the start of a presentation, when nerves tend to run high and out of control. This establishes a more effective pace for our mind and allows our mind to free itself from the breakneck, frenetic pace. Like most of trial advocacy, this eventually becomes second nature.

In our introduction we discussed the zone, where trial lawyers function optimally by focusing on a trial to the exclusion of the rest of the world. To perform in that zone, among other things, we commit to our client's story and thoroughly prepare and practice. We also, however, keep our nerves in check so we concentrate on the task at hand, ignore our inner critic and operate effectively in this zone.

VI.

EXPLORING POINT OF VIEW

"Could a greater miracle take place than for us to look through each other's eyes for an instant?"
— Henry David Thoreau

"You never really understand a person until you consider things from his point of view – until you climb into his skin and walk around in it."
— To Kill a Mockingbird

INTRODUCTION

Good writers and storytellers recognize the value and effectiveness of narrating stories through different points of view. They understand that the perspective of a story determines in large part what and how the audience learns from the story. Storytellers thus utilize different points of view to allow the audience to relate uniquely to the story, gain valuable perspectives and identify with different narrators.

The most commonly used points of view are the first or third person, or some variation thereof, perhaps because we learn them as children and recognize them most easily. With some exceptions, most lawyers in the courtroom use the third person.

The reasons for this vary. At times lawyers simply refuse to walk a mile in the shoes of clients or witnesses. This of course, particularly when dealing with clients, can unfortunately create distance between the lawyer and client because it restricts the client's story at trial by limiting it to the third person point of view. Understandably, many lawyers do not feel comfortable trying to pull off the story presentation in any point of view except the third person.

Other lawyers, though skilled enough to present a story in the first person, view a first person presentation as unpersuasive in a courtroom for one of several reasons, not the least of which is that it may lack credibility by coming off as acting, or over the top. We explore and discuss this in more detail later.

The purpose of this book is not to advocate telling stories in court in a way that is unnatural, uncomfortable or in any way unbecoming of a lawyer. However, there is a tremendous benefit gained from exploring different story points of view, certainly for purposes of brainstorming a case, and, often for actually presenting a story at trial.

Short of telling a client's story in a manner that is uncomfortable for lawyers and seemingly, perhaps, odd to jurors, we can effectively expand our use of different points of view by learning to develop and defend different points of view. Once we explore and develop a story from a different point of view, we learn to defend that point of view in our storytelling, which is a kissing cousin to the idea that we always stay true, when presenting our story at trial, to our case theory. After discussing some exercises to explore different points of view, we discuss its applicability to lawyers and how it can specifically help us most effectively prepare and present our client's story.

EXERCISES

We first look at narratives through the first person, and eventually layer in the six senses. We start with a well-known movie or piece of literature. Later, we will use this exercise with a case specific problem. Keep in mind we do this exercise in the first person through the eyes of several characters, one at a time and in the same story, to most effectively and thoroughly brainstorm a case for trial.

While a group stands in a circle under the direction of a group leader, each person tells a portion of a story from the first person point of view of a single character. The leader directs the group to focus on a specific point in time in an important scene in the story. The leader then prompts each person to add a few sentences in the first person and from the same character in the story.

Much like the Advance/Color tool, the group should freeze the story somewhat in time, so as not to get ahead of the rest of the group. The leader then prompts each person in the group, as they go around the circle, to tell us what the character sees, hears, tastes, feels, smells, and thinks. The leader prompts each person with one of the six senses in random order as they relate the story from the first person point of view.

After the group fleshes out a specific part of the story, the leader then advances the story in time, again assigning random senses as the group continues to flesh out the same character's point of view. This process repeats as the leader moves the story through most or all significant parts of the story.

Interestingly, senses such as taste and smell are often omitted from stories, but the group will productively use those senses, as well as the more obvious senses of sight, hearing, feeling and thought, to create and develop a lush story. Inevitably the group creates a story with a depth that far exceeds the story that had been imagined during a standard brainstorming process. Particularly when repeating this exercise and telling the same story from the point of view of several characters, the exercise adds significant, previously unexplored insight into the case.

After concentrating on telling a story from one point of view, the group takes those lessons learned and collaborates to tell the same story from several points of view, including inanimate objects and other concepts. This exercise allows the participants to tell the same story from different, unique points of view including characters, inanimate objects and other concepts, such as emotions. The leader should encourage participants to take the viewpoints of inanimate objects, emotions and other concepts to understand the value of viewing a case from those different, albeit slightly unusual, angles. Like the previous exercise, we do this exercise initially by using a well-known movie or piece of literature, and subsequently by using an actual case.

During this new exercise, five or six participants line up facing an audience, for lack of a better word, and each person first chooses a character, object or emotion. Each person starts by briefly introducing themselves and stating who or what they represent in the story. One at a time, each person then reveals part of the story through a short monologue from their point of view. As in the previous exercise focusing on the first person/senses, the leader directs the participants to reveal their point of view at important, specific parts of the story.

The participants randomly put their foot forward to signal to the other story tellers when they are ready to add to the story. They then share part of the story from their point of view. This process fleshes out the story and demonstrates that any concept, including people, objects and emotions, will meaningfully add depth to a story and provide valuable brainstorm fodder for presenting the story in court.

Several other exercises also help lawyers recognize and develop the skill of using different points of view. For instance, one person in a group acts as an anchor newscaster by briefly introducing a fictitious or real case story. They subsequently call upon other newscasters out in the field. Those newscasters stay on topic and interview different people associated with the case who can lend their point of view to the story. In addition to recognizing and utilizing different points of view, these exercises teach lawyers how to defend a point of view.

For an exercise that focuses more specifically on defending a point of view, three or four people sit in the front of the room and they introduce themselves as world renowned experts in a particular field. A moderator then takes questions from audience members about the audience members' problems. Each expert then draws on their expertise and offers advice to solve the problem from the point of view of their expertise. While this somewhat silly exercise generally draws quite a few hearty laughs, the participants gain a great understanding of defending a point of view.

During another exercise, a group looks at life on a safari and each person develops and defends the point of view of a different animal with a goal of creating empathy and sympathy for themselves, given their need to brutally kill and consume other animals. The first narrative starts with the need of a smaller animal to eat other animals and ends with their untimely and unwelcome demise at the hands of another, larger animal. The new animal, starting as assassin, then reveals its point of view to show the need to eat the previous animal to survive. Each animal's point of view develops sympathy, before they are eaten by a larger animal.

RECOGNIZING THE AVAILABLE POINTS OF VIEW

Similar to the exploration of emotions, the exploration of a story through different points of view better prepares us to persuasively present a story in court. Novels and stories commonly use the third person ("She said...," "John went to....") point of view as either omniscient or limited. The third person is often the easiest, most convenient and natural way to narrate a story, in part because it offers the narrator wide latitude of insight and the ability to relate intimate feelings and details from several characters and angles.

Particularly in the third person omniscient point of view, the narrator has great latitude in rotating among a variety of characters and broadly delving into the intimate details, beliefs and feelings of those characters. The third person limited point of view restricts the narrator to the intimate details, feelings and point of view of one character. Incidentally, with few exceptions, lawyers most often use some variation of the third person point of view in court.

Storytellers also use the first person and/or the first person plural ("I went...," "We walked...."). Used both in literature and everyday narration, it relates a *personal* story describing a past event. While not offering the varied insights and personal feelings of the third person, the first person when used effectively draws the audience uniquely, deeply and intimately into the mind of the narrator. While used sparingly in court (for better and worse - we will address both sides later), the value of exploring a story from our client's and different character's first person point of view is tremendously productive and often leads us to depths of the story we would not otherwise unearth. Incidentally, many best-loved pieces of literature and movies use the first person.

An even less traditional and more infrequently used approach in court is the point of view through the "eyes" of something other than a person, perhaps an inanimate object or emotion. While much debated, the willingness and ability to explore a story not just through the eyes of characters but also through the "eyes" and unique vantage point of things other than characters is a productive brainstorming tool which often produces good results in terms of persuasive courtroom storytelling.

To say something does not have "eyes" or other senses does not relegate that thing as being useless to a case. In fact, many "things" associated with our cases offer a unique vantage point and "story" from which we garner valuable information for our story at trial. Significantly, the list of points of view other than people is virtually endless and boundless.

Perhaps this sounds a bit surprising, yet to some extent, all lawyers, whether they recognize it or not, brainstorm virtually every case by exploring points of view using this method. We visit a scene, referring at least momentarily to a place where the story of the case occurred, or we brainstorm a case by scouring scene photographs to help find out what happened. Consciously or not, we are exploring the case from the point of view of something *other than a person,* and we creatively use these points of view, of objects, emotions and all non people, to thoroughly and effectively prepare a story for trial.

The second person point of view, albeit used sparingly in literature and storytelling, also deserves mention ("You walked...,""You will think, perhaps..."). The second person is unusual, difficult to master in literature and relatively odd in everyday storytelling, yet it does have a place in the courtroom.

EFFECTIVE BRAINSTORMING:
EXPLORING THE POINTS OF VIEW OF YOUR STORY

We brainstorm different points of view before trial to explore our story creatively, exhaustively and intimately. It is not enough to simply list facts that support or contradict our theory. For instance, it is not enough in William Smith's case to say, "He didn't have the drugs, and here are the facts in support thereof...." This simplistic effort appeals predominantly to Aristotle's logos portion of persuasion.

Many trial stories appear straightforward and simple at face value, yet most have underpinnings, motivations and depth we do not always seek or acknowledge. The search for the heart and depth of our story involves exploring the relatively unlimited points of view that lie therein.

After a verdict, when jurors discuss deliberations and what *they* found important to the case, they often note case issues that the lawyers never presented in court, or for that matter, explored during the brainstorming process. Many of these issues seem a bit far afield, if not completely irrelevant, to lawyers. However, many of these issues might have been explored, prepared and better presented through a brainstorm that thoroughly examined the story's different points of view. This includes the point of view of the client, all witnesses, and where productive, inanimate objects.

Just as each witness undoubtedly has unique, complex and oftentimes changing emotions, they also have a unique point of view. Each witness' involvement shades their narration in unique hues and at times entirely different colors. The story they paint depends on their viewpoint.

Recognizing differing viewpoints helps lawyers accurately tell jurors in opening statement what to expect of witnesses, including why the jurors should or should not believe them. Moreover, in preparing cross-examinations, lawyers will have a better idea of how to cross-examine witnesses and what to expect from a witness *on the witness stand*. Recognizing where the witness is coming from better prepares lawyers to tell their client's story as it relates to other versions likely to be painted by different witnesses.

Looking at a case through the eyes of other witnesses by using the point of view exercises discussed above involves more than merely looking at the witness' emotional assessment and factual statement. Indeed, emotional and factual assessments are helpful and necessary, but they are only part of a character's point of view.

We cannot always and with one hundred percent accuracy, attribute emotions or point of view to a character on the basis of statements and/or interviews, nor can we be certain the witness' testimony will be consistent with *our* assessment. Yet the process of creatively brainstorming point of view by running through different scenarios often does reveal new discoveries, deeper assessments and helpful estimations. Consistent with the *purpose* of brainstorming, we will better represent our client and more persuasively present their story. Like good chess players, we consider all opportunities, strategies, possibilities and vulnerabilities, and inevitably gain fodder for trial throughout the process.

During this creative process, lawyers must act unlawyerly. We should ignore the muscles in our brain that insist on controlling a search only for right and wrong answers. Rather, we access the muscles in our brain developed through improv that accommodate and foster spontaneity and openness. Through exploration and possibility, together with factual and emotional assessments which shift as we explore, we stand in a character's shoes and explore points of view.

After developing a point of view, we learn to defend that viewpoint even when it is not advantageous to our client or supportive of our theory. While we of course more easily defend points of view beneficial to our theory, the good trial lawyer, like the expert chess player assessing a chess board, recognizes the strengths and weaknesses from both sides of the courtroom. Sometimes a point of view is at odds with our theory. However, as devil's advocate, we recognize and defend it to more effectively present *our* story. Because the jurors' feelings, perceptions and opinions matter most, we brainstorm by honestly and accurately recognizing all possible points of view, both favorable and unfavorable.

Point of view options: UTILIZING POINT OF VIEW AT TRIAL

THIRD PERSON

Perhaps the natural comfort level most people have telling stories in the third person explains why it is the most commonly used point of view in court. The ease and comfort with which we relate stories in the third person serves to enhance its persuasive effect because lawyers often lack confidence relating stories through other, more unnatural points of view. Certainly jurors can read a lack of confidence in the story we try to sell, and with few exceptions, what comes naturally will usually be most persuasive.

Many lawyers also use the third person to the exclusion of all other points of view because of its obvious strengths, advantages and flexibility. For instance, the lawyer can take advantage of an omniscient perspective by shifting from one character to another and freely and openly revealing and presenting intimate thoughts, feelings and emotions of different characters on several levels. This allows the storyteller to present a story from an unlimited number of angles and in great depth, to the extent permitted by the evidence and reasonable inferences to be drawn.

From the perspective of most jurors, as they internally create a story upon hearing the evidence, they perhaps appreciate a story told in the third person as it is most familiar to them, and the point of view they likely use most often themselves.

FIRST PERSON

The first person point of view has advantages and disadvantages and must be used with caution considering the story, the lawyer's skills, the audience and most importantly, its persuasive effect. While most often narrated through the client's eyes, we can use the first person through the eyes of any character in a story.

Jurors are most familiar with and perhaps expect third person courtroom presentations. Other points of view including the first person can come across as unusual and perhaps as an attempt to feed them with the wrong utensil. Lawyers must cautiously avoid causing discord between jurors and lawyer, or between the jurors and the client and/or client's story.

Will a jury throw tomatoes at a lawyer who unsuccessfully tells a story using the first person? Probably not, but they might consider it as somewhat of a gimmick because they expect a more traditional presentation. Might jurors view it as an entertaining performance that attempts to distract them from the "real" issues in the case? Possibly, and if they say, "That was sure entertaining," and then side with our opponent, having disbelieved us and disregarded the character's portrayal, we have not effectively persuaded them.

Indeed, acting and lawyering differ. An actor attempts to accurately and believably portray someone else and hopefully create a believable character for the audience. When the audience finds the character believable, the actor has successfully and credibly done the job. A lawyer's task differs and we previously noted some significant differences between actors and lawyers (See Chapter V Emotional Range).

In the courtroom, credibility does not mean convincing jurors the lawyer is someone else nor should a lawyer judge success necessarily on credibly portraying different characters. Rather, a lawyer advocates while drawing upon acting skills. To be successful, the jurors must see us as credible.

In some senses, we put on a *show* during a trial, but with a verdict at stake, lawyers must not lose sight of the fact that a trial is really a *competition.* A behind the back pass in basketball garners significant applause, "oohs and aahs!" But the question is, will the fancy pass contribute to a win? Like a trial, a basketball game is a competition, not a show.

To the extent we use the first person in court, we should accurately portray characters. When portraying characters inaccurately and unfairly in the first person, perhaps we will do so to the detriment of our credibility and necessarily to our client's detriment. We want jurors to like us and rely on us for answers, and in the end, for the *truth*. If using the first person achieves this result, we succeed. But if jurors do not buy into a first person presentation, we fail by ignoring their sensibilities and expectations.

Putting caution aside, we can use the first person advantageously as an effective tool in trial preparation and presentation. While lacking the omniscience of the third person, the first person point of view can benefit a client's story, whether it be from the point of view of the client or from another character in the story. When done well, presenting in first person creates a unique bond between the jurors and the narrator, sacrificing omniscience for the development of a special relationship between jurors and narrator.

Through books, film and other experiences outside the courtroom, we know the powerful feeling of being sucked into the life and intimate feelings of effective first person narration. As the narrator evolves, we likewise evolve emotionally and otherwise as they take us by the hand and lead us into their unique experiences. We sit alongside that character on a rollercoaster and intimately explore their experiences. At times our values, expectations and emotions morph into those of the narrator.

Using the first person in court, we create this same effect by getting jurors intimately involved in a story through the eyes of a first person narrator. Through this intimate connection we grip the jurors, put them in the narrator's shoes and align them with the narrator. When successful, jurors will understand the narrator's point of view, empathize intimately with our case and hopefully reach a favorable verdict.

After deciding to use the first person for all or part of a courtroom presentation, a lawyer should carefully prepare and practice those portions.

BYPASSING THE BRAIN ENROUTE TO THE BLOODSTREAM: INCORPORATING THE "SIX" SENSES INTO POINT OF VIEW

To help our story persuade jurors based on *their* experiences, we incorporate the six senses into different points of view and connect with jurors in a visceral, palpable and immediate way. By using the senses, our story bypasses the jurors' brains en route to their bloodstream as we create contextual elements to which they respond. Their response might be mental, or possibly even physical. Regardless, our story becomes more persuasive when it fits in with their view of the world based on their past experiences.

We reference six senses even though science acknowledges and we commonly refer only to five senses that process information: vision, hearing, touch, smell and taste. While each of these five senses has its own imagination and memory bank, our mental faculties also comprise a sense, of sorts. Thus, we also use this sixth sense, including our thoughts and/or emotional feelings, to make our storytelling more palpable.

Each of the "five" senses has a path leading to a specific part of our brain. When we stimulate a sense, the information is retrieved, collected and taken to a specific part of the brain where it is stored. Our brains then create a memory of the information.

Though we do not often think of our olfactory sense as the sense by which we live our lives, arguably it evokes as much or more memory than any other sense. Our olfactory bulb connects to the brain's limbic system, an area of the brain closely aligned with memory and feeling. Our sense of smell operates consciously and unconsciously, while we are sleeping or awake, to recall memories and influence mood.

When walking around on a daily basis our olfactory sense continuously evokes memory. We note the smells of showers, bacon, coffee or a loved one, as well as the smells of different rooms, hallways, offices, perfumes or fried food. Smells constantly inundate our mind and evoke memories of past experiences. This stimulation takes us back to specific times and places.

Likewise, looking at photographs brings us to specific times and places, and of course, hearing songs will do the same, perhaps bringing us back to high school days or earlier. The smell of pizza to a hungry customer makes (actually literally and physically according to some) that person's mouth water. In each case, the photo, song and pizza evokes memories and brings prior experiences to life in an immediate sense.

On another level, memories and past experiences indelibly attach themselves to specific and powerful emotions. The smell of the entry way to work might evoke despair, fear or relief, depending on that person's work experiences and job satisfaction. The notes of a song or a photograph can likewise evoke specific emotional memories.

In court we recreate unique experiences persuasively by remembering events through the senses and the stimuli associated with those experiences. The story comes alive in an immediate way for the jurors, making the story believable and memorable, particularly when the jurors' past experiences jive with our use of the senses.

Let's go back to Mr. Murphy's story after he was pulled over and got out of his car. Now we interject the technique of using the senses to make the scene come alive.

"After stepping out of his car, Mr. Murphy feels the gravel under his feet as he stands looking at the two troopers approaching him. Annoyed that he had been pulled over in the first place, he can see the quickly spinning red and blue cherry lights on top of the squad. A spot light shines from the driver's side of the squad into his eyes, causing him to squint slightly, so all he can see is the outline of the two troopers. His ears are bombarded by the sounds of officers barking orders, most of which are inaudible, as the orders are drowned out and overwhelmed by the sounds of constant traffic rushing by, which make a loud swishing sound. To add to the confusion, in the background he hears dispatchers and officers speaking over the radio. His nose picks up a scent emanating out from under the hood of the police car, which smells like the moist smell of burning coolant. The rest of his body stiffens, unsure whether he should move or not. He thinks it best to ask what is going on, but because he is too nervous his tongue freezes - he swishes his tongue around his mouth in an attempt to loosen up, but all he can taste is something akin to dry cotton...."

Through the six senses we make the image and story come alive and create a bond between Murphy and the jurors. As we intertwine the story, the senses and common human experience, we present a story, and an *experience*, the jurors can share in. It is alive, palpable and more immediate, and the jurors can actually walk in the shoes of Mr. Murphy by instinctively relating to his experience. We call upon jurors to empathize and identify with our case because they have perhaps experienced something similar, perhaps even vicariously, and they can identify with the experience.

Like the "Advance-Color-Emotion," tool we choreograph this technique with our theory to highlight or augment important scenes to create empathy and good memory.

NO EYES BUT A UNIQUE VANTAGE

The value of telling a story in court from the point of view of something other than a person, perhaps an object or emotion, is debatable. Like the first person point of view, it is artsy, innovative and entertaining, but we must again assess at the end of the day whether and to what extent it persuades jurors to decide a case in your client's favor.

Brainstorming a story from the viewpoint of something other than a person undeniably has tremendous value. The point of view of objects or emotions often offers something unique and not easily, if at all, revealed or accessed through a character's point of view. Thus, we take advantage of the unique perspective of an object by fusing that vantage point into the more traditional third person omniscience.

We diligently prepare cases by investigating and personally viewing scenes of a story. Physical scenes and objects devoid of characters undoubtedly reconstruct and tell part of the story. In many instances, a story falls into place and gains context when we creatively and critically read the scene and absorb the existence, placement and condition of those objects.

Objects can reveal who, what, when, where, how and why. Incidentally, in defending a criminal case where the accused was never at the crime scene, one must still examine the scene thoroughly as part of the story of the case. Objects in a home garbage can, for instance, tell a story. Those objects reveal a history of days, weeks or months and their condition tells a unique story. From top to bottom the contents can reveal sequencing and in some instances a specific timeline of events. From the specific point of view of each object, we contextualize a story and garner a unique perspective including story reconstructions that include revelations about the characters. Much of this vantage point cannot be duplicated or shared by any character. Then, using the "Advance-Color-Emotion" technique, we look more critically at each object in the can and delve deeper into the intensity of the story by brainstorming a case below the surface of scenes and photos. Enlightened by the point of view of an object, we support our theory.

To what end do we tell all or part of our story at trial from the point of view of an object? We need only remember that at trial, we do not only entertain, we must persuade.

SECOND PERSON

At first glance, the second person point of view seems unusual for the courtroom because the narrator uses the "you" format to tell a story to a protagonist or other character. While unusual, the second person does have benefits as the "you" for whom the story is intended becomes personally engaged in the story. The idea of a lawyer referring to jurors as "You…." to tell a story is unusual and odd. And practically, of course, we are not permitted to make jurors the protagonists or other characters in our story.

We can however get jurors and witnesses actively engaged in the story through the second person. When done properly we implore witnesses and jurors to place themselves into the story, if in a limited manner.

During cross-examination we often try to get the witness to "go with us" as we tell our story. Consciously or even unconsciously, a witness often stays with you and in the moment when using the second person point of view, and ideally, the present tense.

Digressing for a moment, we note the power and distinct advantage of the present tense. The present tense creates and encourages immediacy, intimacy and at times heightened drama because the narrator, characters and audience simultaneously experience a story in the here and now. When stories have an unknown outcome, the present tense might increase the dramatic effect. Any story, whether in opening, cross-examination, direct-examination or closing argument, benefits from using the present tense.

Using the second person, we can implore jurors to jump into a story, at least in a limited manner. For example, in arguing for the acquittal of William Smith, we get jurors to understand how arresting Officer Jones may have acted overzealously. We do so by deftly shifting from the third person to the second. It goes something like this:

"Officer Jones was out on Madison Street trying to get rid of crime. As an officer, *you're* out there, trying to do *your* best, and *you're* trying to pay attention to everything that's going on around you. But *you* can't see everything, so at times, *you're* going to rely on what others tell you, all the while knowing, *all you want* to do is make an arrest...."

Moving from the third person into the second person, we allow jurors, at least for a limited time and purpose, to become actively involved in the story, and through the present tense, we make the story more immediate. Of course we can do this with our client or any other character.

The use of the second person in instruction manuals also suggests how we can use it in court. Specifically, we use it to guide jurors in tasks such as deliberations by imploring them, in closing argument for instance, to pay special attention to specific jury instructions. Using the "you...," format we tell them,"...You twelve people can make this situation right for my Mr. Smith when you go back and deliberate...."

Most often we do not force feed conclusions to the jurors because we let evidence speak for itself and allow jurors to draw their own conclusions. We know jurors will more vigorously defend conclusions when they reach them on their own. When a movie ends with a couple riding off on a horse into the sunset, the director empowers the audience to easily conclude the couple lives happily ever after. The audience receives only ninety percent of the story but readily and easily concludes the unspoken, final ten percent. Similarly, we abide by this concept in court.

MIX AND MATCH: CHANGING POINTS OF VIEW

Given the inherent benefits and limitations of different points of view, we should mix and match by shifting in and out of them. Often we switch from the commonly used third person to either first or second person, but the options and combinations are endless and we are limited only by our imaginations on a story by story, case by case basis. We decide which point of view to use for each snippet of the story based, among other things, on the story content, emotions and case theory.

Above we demonstrated how we switch from the third person to the second person to support our theory. By setting a scene with an effective transition, we can seamlessly shift points of view to allow jurors to stand in the shoes of different characters to best suit our theory.

We can also shift from the third person, for instance, into the first person, if we want to take advantage of the first person for selected parts of the story. To do so we again slide seamlessly from the third into the first, albeit for a well-defined purpose and limited time, to interject the power of the first person.

We do so in William Smith's story for instance before his arrest as he walks down the street, immediately after seeing the police. We start in the third person, move to the first person (as noted by the quotation marks) and then move back into the third person. Immediately before and after the inserted quotation marks we insert a communicative pause, either alone or in conjunction with another transitional tool:

"As William walked down Madison Street with his friends, basketball in hand, he heard the slight screech of car tires, so he glanced over his shoulder and saw a police car. He did not know what to think. 'Why are the police pulling up here so quickly? I don't see anything wrong around here and no one I'm with has done anything wrong. They must be here on another call. I'm not gonna pay attention to them, I'm gonna go play some ball.' William kept walking westbound on Madison Street toward the playground."

By combining points of view, we allow jurors to see the story from the first person point of view of an innocent man. We buttress our change in point of view with a transition on each end to highlight what is otherwise a simple change in language.

When uncomfortable using solely the first person, we use a third person omniscient point of view to garner many of the same benefits. To demonstrate the same thoughts of an innocent man when he sees the police car, we simply replace our first person segment and transpose it into the third person omniscient format:

"He didn't know why the police were pulling up so quickly. He didn't notice anything wrong and no one he was with had done anything wrong. He assumed they were there on another call...." Through the omniscient point of view we create an effect similar to that of the first person.

VII.

STRUCTURING AND SEQUENCING THE STORY

"Some of the best openings have come from the end of Act 1, end of Act 2, and even the end of the entire script. Look through your story and label the 5 most interesting scenes. Maybe one of them should be your opening scene."

— Screenwritingu.com

INTRODUCTION

Whether telling a story in opening statement, closing argument, cross examination or direct examination, we need to sequence our story most persuasively. The sequence can and will make a significant difference in how jurors digest and understand the story. A chronological story is effective, but only one of several persuasive ways to tell the story.

Trial lawyers too often tell a client's story chronologically simply because the easiest, most accessible way to prepare and tell the story is to line up facts in the order in which they unfolded. During closing argument this method is often coupled with a rehash of the witnesses' testimony, during which lawyers individually line up and recap each witness' testimony. This lineup and rehash process is certainly easy to prepare, but as easy as it is to prepare, it is often also unpersuasive. It is not a true closing argument, but rather a "summation." Incidentally, this explains why lawyers should make arguments and not merely give summations. When a lawyer stands up to argue a case by saying, "Let's review the witness' testimony...,"we can only imagine many jurors thinking, "Let's Not! We just listened to the testimony for two weeks." Indeed, a traditional rehash of the witnesses' testimony most often lacks luster, persuasiveness and any real creativity.

Putting the old rehash aside, a straight chronological story can be persuasive and effective. After all, many jurors are accustomed to hearing chronological stories, and similarly, we naturally and often tell stories chronologically. It is sensible, smooth and easily digested. So certainly, it is not a bad method of presenting a story in court.

The issue, however, is one of creativity and persuasiveness. More specifically, can we creatively design a story sequence to not only catch the jurors' eyes and attention, but to perhaps entertain *and* persuade? How can we most effectively sequence a story to optimize the inherent drama in a story? And in the absence of drama, can we create drama for emphasis?

POWERFUL BOOKENDS: PRIMACY AND RECENCY

We start with two useful staples of rhetoric, primacy and recency. With the audience's tendency to pay close attention to and remember what they hear first and last, we seize the inherent courtroom drama by carefully considering and crafting our primacy and recency - how we start and finish a story.

Let's note first that we do not want to begin a story in court with a salutation that falls within the outdated but common tradition of legalese nonsense. In opening statement or closing argument, the legalese salutation usually involves something like this: While nodding to the judge, "Thank you, your honor, thank you Ms. Bratton (while nodding to opposing counsel), and I thank my client, Mr. Smith for the privilege of representing him. And last but not least, thank you 12 ladies and gentleman for sitting attentively and listening to all the evidence in this case. You have done a wonderful job...." On direct examination, it will usually go something like this: "In a loud clear voice would you please state your name for the record and spell your last name for the court reporter...." And of course on cross examination: "Mr. Witness, my name is Joe Lawyer and I would like to ask you a few questions if you do not mind. Please let me know if there is anything you do not understand...." Blah, blah, blah, blah.

Many lawyers use these traditional introductions in court to begin what is supposedly a story. They blindly and thoughtlessly use these legalistic, formulaic introductions, perhaps because a law school professor encouraged them to do so. Unfortunately, these introductions fail to take advantage of and optimize one of two of the most opportune times to persuade jurors, the start of a story.

Most trials have inherent drama. This partially explains modern culture's obsession with fictional court television shows, and more recently, real life courtroom drama. Admittedly some cases are inherently more interesting than others because of the crime, accident or story involved, yet every trial to some extent is spicy and dramatic in its own way, undoubtedly with certain parts of the trial being more dramatic than others.

As advocates, in addition to taking advantage of inherent drama, we can also *create* drama during a trial. In either situation, we take dramatic moments, whether inherent or created, and use them most powerfully and persuasively.

In a criminal trial for instance we consider the inherent drama. Assume you represent Mr. Parker who is charged with a well-publicized homicide. During the prosecutor's opening statement they effectively lay out their case, including gruesome details, and of course, fingers pointed at Mr. Parker. Upon finishing the opening, the prosecutor sits down and silence grips the courtroom. During the silence, the jurors stare at Mr. Parker disgustingly as if he is the devil. The ill-will toward Mr. Parker is so thick you can cut it with a knife. The judge then looks over at you and says, "Does the defense wish to make an opening statement?" After this invitation there is silence again.

This is courtroom drama. During the ensuing silence, Mr. Parker sits in the throngs of an emotional, serious, and in some ways, exciting conflict. After the judge invites you to make an opening statement, the jurors now stare at you, perhaps wondering what you could *possibly* say to get them to even *consider* anything but a guilty verdict. The jurors' focus intensifies on you as you stand to speak. Before you utter a word, the tension thickens.

This drama is unique. During the remainder of the trial, it will be difficult if not impossible to get all the jurors to focus in unison on your presentation. Most jurors will have the usual lapses in attention and unfortunately, some might even doze off during trial. But for at least this limited moment, they sit on the edge of their seats paying close attention to you. To the jurors and opposing counsel, there is suspense. The jurors expect something from you.

Imagine at this dramatic moment, after gruesome details and finger pointing, you stand up and out of your mouth comes "May it please this honorable court. Counsels for the Government, my client, Mr. Parker and of course you all, Ladies and gentlemen of the jury, I have the privilege of representing Mr. Parker and we thank you in advance for your service. The job you have is a difficult one...Blah, Blah, Blah ...."

Through this canned salutation you forfeited the opportunity to take advantage of a unique, riveting moment that happens but once during the trial. You deflated that moment with a legalistic salutation that did not take advantage, in any way, of the courtroom drama. The one shot was wasted.

More importantly, you wasted a unique chance to capitalize on a dramatic moment and immediately *advance your client's story and case theory* in the eyes of the jurors. This is an ideal opportunity squandered.

Opening statement is arguably the most important part of a trial and we must take advantage. It should be powerful and persuasive. Some people even suggest an inordinately high number of jurors might perhaps decide a case after the openings. This may or may not be true. Regardless, an opening statement should be presented as your chance to *win* the case. We should open with fervor and commitment, as if it was our *last* chance to speak for our client. Primacy should exceed canned salutations. We should take advantage of drama to the benefit of our client throughout the trial, including voir dire, opening statement, cross-examination, direct examination and closing argument.

When a significant witness testifies in the above homicide prosecution of Mr. Parker, direct examination ends with drama and silence. After the witness pointed a finger at Mr. Parker and described in vivid detail how Mr. Parker shot and killed an innocent person, the judge looks to the defense table and says, "Counsel, cross-examination?" You are again faced with another unique, "one shot" dramatic moment that must be used advantageously.

Direct examination likewise presents a unique chance to use primacy to seize drama. A client's testimony, in particular, typically elicits a heightened degree of the jurors' attention because the client is the person most affected by a lawsuit or criminal case and the jurors have heard about them in depth, often repeatedly, during the course of a trial. Thus, when that witness takes center stage, jurors will likely pay close attention.

Heightened attention and scrutiny brings heightened drama together with good opportunities to capitalize on that drama. Hence, the old, overused phrase, "Would you please state your name for the record and spell your last name for the court reporter...," simply does not cut it. Why ask the witness to "state their name" when the jurors and court reporter have heard it a hundred times or more during the course of several days, weeks or months? More importantly, in using canned, legalese primacy, we miss a valuable chance to effectively reinforce pertinent issues, preferably issues central to the client's story and supportive of our theory. On direct examination, a better opening question is "Mr. Smith, why are you here testifying today?"

We use a simple method to most persuasively and fully take advantage of primacy and recency. We also use this method to *create* and take advantage of drama during the trial. Let's first use this method to create effective primacy. Using a communicative pause and silence it goes like this.

While representing Mr. Parker, we prepare to make an opening statement after the prosecutor sits down. The judge then invites our opening statement with the perfunctory, "Opening statement on behalf of the defense?" We should not stand up abruptly and speak immediately as we walk out in front of the jurors, as if we can make the jurors forget what they just heard. It is tempting to do so. However, an abrupt start does not take advantage of courtroom drama nor does it effectively and meaningfully set up what we are about to say.

Rather than standing quickly and speaking almost immediately, we do the opposite after the invitation. We stand up deliberately, if somewhat slowly, and move away from counsel table confidently. We walk toward a preselected spot in the courtroom from which we will begin our opening statement. We probably will not deliver the entire opening statement from this spot. Rather, we will use the courtroom space as discussed in chapter IX.

When we get to our spot, we pause again and stand still for a few seconds until we can feel the jurors' gaze warm upon us. Then we begin speaking. This does not, to be sure, recommend we stand up excessively slowly and melodramatically, causing jurors to think we are oddballs. Nor do we stand in front of jurors on our spot for an extended period that makes them uncomfortable. However, we use a communicative pause and its accompanying silence to seize the drama.

Incidentally, we also use this method before beginning a cross-examination, particularly of a critical witness. After the judge's usual invitation of, "Cross-examination, counsel..," we follow the same steps to best seize the drama. Whether during opening statement, cross examination or any other part of the trial, the *content* of our primacy must not be a let-down. It must be powerful and worthy of our set-up. What better primacy on a cross examination, for instance, than "We can agree you are a *convicted felon...*," with appropriate emphasis, of course, on *convicted felon*.

We also pay special attention to *recency*: the way we finish a particular segment at trial. When we finish an opening, cross or direct, we do not necessarily have the same drama that is built in to our primacy. The drama of a story varies and the unique drama of primacy, perhaps due to its basis in expectation, suspense and surprise, will dwindle as the story progresses.

Notwithstanding fluctuating and dissipating drama, we recognize the importance of recency and note our ability to *create* drama using a method similar to that used in our primacy. We do not want a story to simply fizzle out at the end. Rather, we want to end on a high note and get off the stage with power, leaving something that will stick with jurors. As an actor might say, we will "leave something in the room."

When we sit down to finish a segment of trial, we deposit something, whether a thought, emotion, feeling, or preferably, all of the above into the well of the courtroom and the jury box. Much like the effect created by a gunslinger in an old western movie, after a ubiquitous entrance into and subsequent exit from a tavern, the departure leaves everyone cognizant, and almost overwhelmed, by his presence. During the hush after his departure, his persona is palpable.

With this in mind, we want to save some good material for our recency in order to get off the stage with power and "leave something in the room." The process is simple. We start the beginning of the end with a communicative pause and then finish with powerful material. Then we pause again and slowly walk to counsel table and sit down. This is how, for instance, we finish an opening statement.

Too often lawyers finish an opening statement with a legalese request of jurors to side with their client, such as,

"...the State will not prove their case beyond a reasonable doubt and we ask that you find the defendant not guilty of murder." This request usually continues with a "thank you," after which counsel immediately turns around, walks back to counsel table and sits down. Worse yet, some lawyers actually begin to turn around *as* they finish their opening and without pause, they abruptly walk away from the jury and sit down. These abrupt departures exhibit a lack of confidence in the ultimate request of the jurors and fail to capitalize on the "sit down" statement. These departures also exhibit a lack of commitment to the client's story, because the story fizzles out weakly and ineffectively, ending not with a "bang but a whimper."

We want powerful primacy, coupled with and setting up equally powerful recency, to best benefit our story. When preparing to finish our opening, for instance, we introduce "the beginning of the end" with a communicative pause. We remember Miles Davis' notion of the power of notes coming from the silence before and afterward. We pause to set up our recency and create drama by transitioning, capturing the jury's attention and letting them know we are moving into something important. The pause lasts about four to five seconds, though this of course is not set in stone and we will pause intuitively and naturally to the extent that the pause is effective.

After this initial pause we move into our recency with a critical, persuasive part of the story. Then we again use a communicative pause of approximately three to four seconds as we face the jurors to complete the process. Only after this final pause do we turn around, walk slowly back to counsel table and sit down.

Some lawyers feel the need to "thank" the jurors upon completion but this is not necessary. If you insist on doing so, wait until after the final three to four second pause so the sequence would be - pause, recency, pause, "thank you," and then sit down.

This process should not be melodramatic, campy or over the top. We simply use our communicative pause to finish a trial segment powerfully. Of course we use the same technique during voir dire, cross-examination, direct examination and closing argument, to end on a high note and leave something in the room.

Cross-examination in particular offers an opportune time to leave something in the room, especially when finishing a cross-examination of a critical witness. After the recency, grab your notes and walk slowly back to counsel table. Unsure of whether you finished or are simply walking to speak with co-counsel, your recency lingers in the room for several seconds until you sit down and say, "nothing further."

We can likewise milk any important part of our story, at any point during trial, by similarly using a communicative pause, followed by something important, followed by another communicative pause. Like the notes from Miles Davis' trumpet, the silence highlights, emphasizes and "milks" helpful evidence by allowing the evidence to sink deeply into the jurors' minds. Remember that while jurors have down time, they will digest your story and theory.

IN "ORDER" TO PERSUADE

In addition to our primacy and recency, we also thoughtfully and creatively arrange the overall order, or *sequence*, of the story. Stories typically have a beginning, middle and end, or in the vernacular of storytelling, an exposition, building action and denouement.

Using our "Once upon a time" format, we recognized the story backbone. Our story will have a platform, tilt and resolution ie. "Once upon a time...But one day...Until finally....etc." Using our story backbone, we generally acknowledge that we usually tell each part of the story, and according to some conventional wisdom, we need to tell the story in that order. However, while we usually tell all three parts of the story, we do not always do so in that order. We can adjust and modify the sequence of the story to suit our persuasive goals. Indeed, a story should have a beginning, middle and end, but those parts do not necessarily have to come in that order. The important thing is that the storyteller recognize the different parts.

Stories can be told in many ways and story sequences can vary significantly. As a guiding light for court we need only look to the sensibilities of the jurors and how they will best *receive and digest* a story.

In social settings we most naturally and commonly tell stories chronologically. We generally tell and receive most fact patterns in a "start to finish" format, in part, because chronological stories are easily told, understood and digested. Many lawyers do not deviate from this practice in court, and they cannot be faulted, considering the goal of getting jurors instantly, easily and firmly connected to a story. Jurors will easily follow and digest a chronological story.

During cross-examination, we alter a chronological sequence at times to keep the witness off balance. The lawyer's focus, however, remains on how the jurors will best understand, digest and remember the cross examination. Our effective use of transitions ("I want to ask you some questions now about the car, you understand?") allows for us to mix up our cross without losing and confusing jurors. Occasionally lawyers worry that a chronological cross allows the witness to gain an advantage because the witness gets in tune with the lawyer's "plan," but truth be told, a well prepared cross examination leaves no room for any witness to gain an advantage over a prepared cross examiner.

In addition to telling chronological stories, our creativity often beckons that we experiment with different formats and sequences. There are many effective and successful ways to sequence a story and more importantly, to persuade jurors.

For instance, we can start a story with the ending. Think of the intrigue we get when a story begins with, "Our family has broken apart and will never be the same, because we were victimized by a summer in a brutal city...." Rather than using the building action and ensuing conflicts to gather interest and draw the audience into the story, we start the story with its chronological "end." By initially skipping over the traditional "once upon a time," we draw the audience in without any knowledge of characters, conflict, or for that matter, any background information. This sequence uses an opening line that plays on the audience's curiosity to create a thirst for answers. The audience then listens as the story unfolds and satisfies that curiosity. In many instances, this sequence helps the audience immediately identify with the protagonist. We can follow up this introduction with the "Once upon a time" and "But one day" parts of the story.

In the courtroom, for instance, we can use this sequence to draw in jurors by whetting their appetite for the story and solidifying their sense of identification with our client. For Mr. Smith, we might use this technique in opening statement as our primacy: "William Smith's life and college dreams will never be the same since the day he decided to hang around the wrong people...." Through this opening statement primacy we ignite the jurors' curiosity and set the stage for the eventual explanation of *why* his life and dreams will never be the same. We then tell his story and satisfy their appetite as we flash forward and backward.

Using a different fact pattern, perhaps we use a split screen, where we present two separate, seemingly unrelated scenes alongside one another, such as, "While someone was shooting John Fisher on the south side at 65th and Lowe, Mr. Parker was eating dinner with his grandmother across town...."

To sequence a story creatively and effectively, we sift through the story and identify the important scenes. Incidentally, visiting, investigating and scouring the actual scenes from a case before trial is imperative. It bolsters storytelling generally, and in particular, picture painting. On cross examination it also controls witnesses because they know you have *been there* and you cannot be fooled.

Using various scenes as building blocks, we arrange those blocks in different ways so the jurors will easily digest the story. Eventually, we settle on a sequence that best persuades our jurors. Regardless of whether our primacy is from the beginning, middle or end of the story, we want to immediately promote our theory, front-load an important part of the case and cause jurors to identify with our client.

VIII.

SYSTEMATICALLY PERSUASIVE COURTROOM LANGUAGE

INTRODUCTION

Slight differences in expression and emotion can change our message in its entirety. For instance, we can say "I don't know what to expect," in a matter of fact tone of voice. However, the meaning and message changes completely when we say the same words anxiously. The expression further takes on a different meaning depending on whether the "anxiety" is due to the expectation that something good might happen or due to the worry that something bad might happen. As we fine tune our speaking skills, we recognize that the *way* we express ourselves sends a unique message to a listener independent of *what* we say.

But *what* we say, of course, starts with our language, and we acknowledge language as one of the most persuasive and powerful tools in the courtroom. We will discuss the language frequently used in court, language as it should be used in court and how we develop a systematic, persuasive courtroom language.

THE LANGUAGE OF "LAWYERS"

Before law school we were all human beings. We spoke like human beings and our fellow human beings understood our language. We did not use foreign, nonsensical phrases like "burden of proof," "exit the vehicle...," and "preponderance of the evidence" with friends, family or acquaintances. Nor would we ask someone where they are "employed." Indeed, those laughable phrases might have gotten us thrown out of the house or a bar because real human beings do not use that language.

During law school we underwent a transformation. We started regularly responding in conversations, however innocuous, with the inherently argumentative reply of "Yes, but....," and we also started speaking a cryptic and unusual language called legalese. Armed with our new knowledge we communicated on a higher level, in ways mere mortals could not understand. When speaking with friends, family and other "normal" people, they had little if any interest in, nor could they understand, what we were talking about. The legalese was at best ineffective, and at worst, meaningless. While perhaps this language created a comfort level with fellow law students, it also separated us from the population of normal, everyday human beings. Most unfortunately, these normal people included all of our jurors.

The legalese commonly used in court is ineffective, meaningless and certainly unpersuasive. Because language is a most precious gift and courtroom tool, lawyers need a 'lawbotomy' to purge and cleanse them of systematic, unpersuasive legalese. Courtroom language, in particular, should systematically and habitually be carefully crafted, loaded and persuasive.

THE LANGUAGE OF JURORS AND OTHER HUMAN BEINGS

To stop talking like lawyers and lawbotomize ourselves, we revert back to the human beings we were before law school. In the courtroom we need to have people "introduce themselves," rather than "state their names." We need to ask people where they "work," rather than where they are "employed," and we need to show the witness "defense exhibit one" rather than showing "what I have previously marked as defense exhibit number one for purposes of identification." Betting dollars to donuts, we know that in a social setting, if someone asks where you are "employed," and from what "vehicle did you exit..," the conversation would not last long, perhaps just long enough for you to slip off to the bathroom, never to return

In the criminal arena in particular, we need to resist the temptation to jump into the cop-speak that has inundated and become the voice of the criminal justice system. We stop "exiting our vehicle," and revert back to the good old days, in more simpler and humane times, when we used to "get out of our car." Criminal defense lawyers in particular, must not try cases using police terms. Similar to jumping into an opponent's imaginary space, as discussed later, defending a criminal case using cop-speak is akin to playing the game on your opponent's home field.

Jurors do not speak this nonsensical language and it has no place in the courtroom. Perhaps, in some limited circumstances, we use some legal terms to address a judge for the purpose of making an appellate record. But even then, to any extent possible, we should speak like human beings. Arguing that the prosecution "has proven the case beyond a reasonable doubt," or has not "proven their case beyond a reasonable doubt," is no more persuasive with a judge than it is with a jury. It means little or nothing. We should habitually speak in court like human beings because, among other things, unpersuasive legalese belies the strong commitment we otherwise have for our client and their story.

PERSUASIVE THEORY BASED LANGUAGE

After relearning to speak like human beings by lawbotomizing ourselves and eliminating legalese, our next step is to become effective courtroom wordsmiths who use persuasive language that supports our theory. Language is a precious gift only to the extent we take advantage of it by exploring available words and choosing the right fit for our story and our theory.

If necessary, in the matter of ten seconds or so, we easily conjure up several synonyms that *roughly* equate to the word "angry": perturbed, mad, livid, ticked-off, annoyed, irked, and steamed. A lawyer describing someone as "angry," however, needs to find the *right* word. Although similar, each word has a different and distinct connotation, and thus, only one word best suits our story and theory by most accurately describing what we want to say. Words are loaded and we should explore their usage, connotations and net effect.

We test words in our story by taking the time to conjure up and consider several synonyms. In perhaps a few seconds, we have several words available and the wordsmithing begins. We then choose the word that best and most accurately conveys our point and the feeling we try to evoke.

Carefully crafted, persuasive courtroom language propels our story because every word will most appropriately and accurately convey and promote our theory to the jurors. On another level, it demonstrates our commitment to our client. Like the use of the six senses, carefully selected language also implants our case theory directly into the jurors' bloodstream. It operates consciously and subconsciously so our theory bypasses jurors' brains and directly enters their bloodstream.

Let's juxtapose, for example, unpersuasive and persuasive terms. In defending Mr. Parker's criminal homicide case, you have witnesses who will testify he was not there at the time of the shooting. He was across town at his grandmother's house eating dinner. Traditionally, this defense was an "alibi" defense, and lawyers specifically told jurors that Mr. Parker did not commit the homicide because he had an "alibi."

This word, however, does not support his case theory and story. Worse yet, it actually harms his case because an "alibi," consistent with its dictionary definition, connotes and implies that Mr. Parker possibly or likely shot the deceased, and he is now searching for an *excuse* to try and avoid blame and punishment.

By literal definition, alibi means two things. One, an alibi is a *plea* that a person was somewhere other than where the crime was committed. It specifically does not mean the person *was* elsewhere when the crime was committed. Second, and far worse for Mr. Parker, it implies a plausible *excuse* intended to avert blame or punishment. Literally and connotatively, the word alibi does him no favors. It does not drive home the case theory and story that he *was not there* during the shooting.

On some level also, perhaps consciously and/or unconsciously, "alibi" reflects defense counsel's lack of commitment to his defense and a disbelief in his claim of innocence. If anything, the word injects a theory of guilt into the bloodstream of the jurors. How then do we describe the defense to jurors? "He was not there!"

Another example in the criminal context demonstrates how two words, often used haphazardly, serve very different purposes: "victim" and "complaining witness." For good reason most prosecutors regularly use the word "victim" as it connotes "victimization," and thus, inherently calls upon jurors' sympathies, given the assumed trauma and hardship suffered by the "victim." Without any proof, thought or explanation, the term invites jurors to bestow upon that person, sight unseen, sympathy and well-wishes.

Often enough in criminal cases, however, the so-called victim is merely a "complaining witness," a term with a different connotation that makes a world of difference. Unlike a "victim," a "complaining witness," sight unseen and without further explanation, does not inherently invoke the jurors' sympathy. They are a witness "complaining" about something, but there is no connotation of inherent validity to their complaint.

Further, given the sometimes negative connotation of "complain," it might suggest the witness is simply dissatisfied, annoyed and filing a grievance of sorts, without implicitly suggesting the complaint's validity. Many people do not like "complainers," as it often connotes whining or frivolity. If in fact a person cries "Robbery!", but no robbery occurred, that person is not "victim," but merely a complaining witness.

Without belaboring the point, we note a few more courtroom phrases, highlighting the significance of each. When impeaching with an inconsistent statement, the phrases "testimony" and "story" are often misused. "Testimony...," connotes a truth telling function, as opposed to "Your story is...," "You claimed...," or "You allege...," each of which implies the person has not told the truth. When impeaching with an inconsistent statement, your case theory, and more specifically *what* you want the jurors to believe, dictates the appropriate phrase.

Was a suspect at the police station held in an "interview room?" In other words, do we imply the suspect was treated fairly, well fed and well taken care of? Or were they confined to an "interrogation room," connoting, at a minimum, an adversarial, confrontational setting, and perhaps physical abuse and torture?

On a conscious and subconscious level we constantly send signals to jurors based on our language. During cross-examination, for instance, assuming our theory dictates that we create as much distance as possible between a witness and what they saw, we ask how "far" it was, rather than how "close." Cross-examination uniquely allows us the opportunity to put our language and our terms into the mouths of opponents' witnesses. We should take full advantage, particularly by getting the witness in the 'yes' mode and installing our terms repeatedly and at will, often by looping.

Much like using imaginary space as discussed in chapter IX, opposing counsels will often adopt *our* terms and speak our language. After establishing through the witness how "far" something was on cross examination, opposing counsel on redirect examination will often rehabilitate their own witness by adopting your term "far." By doing so, your adversary inevitably, if even subconsciously, lends plausibility and credence to your theory and story.

Incidentally, we also eliminate tag lines from cross examination. We lose, "isn't that correct," "isn't that a fact," "right," "correct," or other common prefixes and suffixes used commonly on cross. These phrases interrupt the story on cross, and by their very nature, are *unnatural* to a story. We want the jury to remember the carefully selected, theory based thread of the examiner, rather than a heap of silly, lawyerly tag lines.

These are just a few examples of the importance of word selection, persuasive courtroom language and how we can most effectively impact jurors through language while telling our story. Creative and selective wordsmithing tells our story most powerfully and often gets our adversaries and their witnesses to adopt our terms, allowing us, on a conscious and subconscious level, to interject our theory into the jurors' bloodstream. Like all good habits of trial practice, we will eventually use effective language with an unconscious capability.

IX.

DEMONSTRATIVE EVIDENCE, BODY LANGUAGE AND COURTROOM PHYSICALITY

INTRODUCTION

To supplement and bolster our story in court we use available physical props, or what some call demonstrative evidence. Legally, demonstrative evidence refers to *anything* we use to aid the trier of fact in understanding the evidence or *anything* we use to help explain the evidence to the trier of fact. We will come back to the word "anything" in a minute. For now we note the limitation on demonstrative evidence – our demonstrative evidence cannot mislead the trier of fact. Traditionally, demonstrative evidence consisted of photographs, diagrams, charts, maps or other tangible evidence, and frequently, many of these things were shown to witnesses, offered into evidence, and at times, if appropriate, sent back with the jurors during deliberation.

We use demonstrative evidence because audiences in general, and jurors are no exception, retain far more information when we combine oral presentations with visuals. Audiences can forget words quickly and easily. But visuals help make our story, and particularly the important parts of our case, memorable for jurors. Few people who watched the O.J. Simpson trial remember much of what was said, yet most remember the glove. On another level, demonstrative evidence aids our effort to make courtroom presentations more entertaining.

Most traditional demonstrative evidence was shown to witnesses, introduced into evidence and at times sent back with jurors for deliberations. However, in presenting our case and telling stories in court, we need to expand this view to include the many other "demonstrative" things that do not fall into this category. For lack of a better word, we call them demonstrative *presentations*. Many demonstrative presentations are never marked as exhibits, shown to witnesses, introduced into evidence or sent back with the jury for deliberations.

As courtroom persuaders, everything we do when we walk into a courtroom should reflect our commitment to our client and their story. There should be a synergy in our courtroom presentation that "demonstrates," if you will, to everyone in the courtroom, including the judge, opposing counsel, and of course most importantly the jurors, our commitment to our client. The concept of demonstrative "presentations" encapsulates all the demonstrative things we do in court, particularly all the presentations that are not offered as evidence, admissible as evidence or shown to any witness. We use these demonstrative presentations, among other things, to highlight good facts of our case, create a good memory of our story and get jurors to sign the appropriate verdict form.

The form of how we present our story, including emotion and body language, is most often more important than the substance. To some extent movie dialogue moves the plot, yet the emotion, special effects, physical surroundings and scenery contribute significantly to making the movie compelling, entertaining and persuasive. Likewise, in court we use physical surroundings, scenery, and special effects to make our story more compelling, entertaining, and persuasive.

To maximize theses effects, however, we must expand our traditional definition of "anything," as this word is used above to define demonstrative evidence. We must use anything and everything available to us to aid the jurors in understanding the evidence and to help explain the evidence. Through powerful language and a broad definition of "anything," we strive to persuade jurors consciously and subconsciously by creatively connecting with them on every level and at each opportunity.

We will not focus on the traditional forms of demonstrative evidence. Rather, we discuss primarily how we use improv to develop and expand demonstrative "presentations," such as body language and invisible courtroom space, often omitted from traditional demonstrative evidence discussions.

EXERCISES TO RECOGNIZE, UTILIZE AND DEVELOP BODY LANGUAGE

Several exercises previously discussed develop an understanding of the importance of body language. Recalling our warm ups, for example, we paired up with an unfamiliar person for several minutes to find out how many things we have in common while relying solely on body language to communicate. We add to those exercises a simple game of catch with an imaginary basketball to get further acclimated to the physicality around us.

Freeze tag, or some variation thereof, is an exercise done while creating short scenes. As a basic variation of freeze tag, two people start a short scene, similar to our warm up scene starts, while the other participants watch. At an undesignated, appropriate time, a third person yells, "freeze!" signaling to the two original people to remain still. The two original participants remain perfectly still until the third person commences a new scene based initially on the frozen body language of the two original participants. The three then continue until a fourth person "freezes" them, creating a new scene again set up based on the body language of the frozen participants. This exercise encourages and creates increased movement with each new scene and the participants recognize and creatively use movement and body language.

Ideally, the scenes continue until the last person creates a scene that involves all of the participants. Two variations on the exercise help to develop focus as well as movement and body language. The first will have the last person involved find an artful way to exit their scene, consistent with the topic of the scene. As each person exits the scenes in the reverse order in which they entered the scene, the scene reverts back swiftly and seamlessly to the previous scene and continues as if it had not been interrupted, or frozen. This pattern continues until only the original two participants remain. The original two participants play out and bring to an end their original scene.

To challenge the participants somewhat, we can throw a sequencing element into the exercise. As the participants exit each scene one at a time, the scene that follows moves ahead significantly in time. For instance, a scene where strangers are meeting each other at a bar skips over to the end of the evening.

To prepare to tell a client's story in court, it is a good practice and challenge to make an entire opening statement while consciously and simultaneously showing the audience everything that you speak of with your hands. Lawyers can then reclaim their ability to speak with their hands naturally, similar to how they did so when they were young kids sharing personal stories. Most often lawyers tell stories outside the courtroom by using their body language, and in particular, their hands like storytellers, rather than lawyers.

Exercises that develop body language and movement, such as "freeze," help lawyers use the invisible space in the courtroom, loosen up and become a blank canvas in terms of body language, now ready to use effective body language in court.

DOES YOUR BODY LANGUAGE INVITE THE JURORS TO LIKE YOUR CLIENT?

Trying a case for a client we actually and genuinely *like* makes the job easier and certainly, on some level, our chances of winning increase. Likewise, our chances increase when we get the jurors, to any extent possible, to actually and genuinely *like* our client. Humanizing a client is a staple of opening statement and this process must be accomplished at every opportunity during the trial.

In some instances, jurors will not hear a word out of your client's mouth unless and until the client testifies. In the meantime, during the entire time your client sits at counsel table, whether a day or a month, jurors inevitably form opinions and make judgments about your client based solely on the client's body language as well as body language exhibited between you and your client.

Do we actually need to genuinely like our client to win a trial? The short answer is 'no', but it certainly helps for obvious reasons. When we genuinely like our client, the attorney-client communications will be better, easier and more productive, and the trial a more enjoyable experience. More importantly, we more naturally portray a positive relationship openly and outwardly through our body language.

Our body language toward our client sends clear signals about our feelings for our client. Those signals can affect judges' and jurors' assessments and alter our client's fate. Preferably, we genuinely like our client, but to the extent that might not be the case, we should adjust our body language carefully so as not to send bad signals to jurors. This might mean putting a hand on a client's shoulder and not brushing them off when they speak to you, as these signals bind themselves inextricably with jurors' feelings for a client.

Imagine yourself as a juror. The judge, most notably, has introduced you to several new people in the social setting of a trial. Naturally, you begin to form opinions about these new people, considering among other things, body language. Given the outwardly adversarial nature of a trial, you likely see some people in the courtroom clearly demonstrate body language that reflects dislike or disdain for others.

Often during a criminal case, for instance, many people in the courtroom physically demonstrate resentment toward the accused. Jurors pick up on these signals and unfortunately perhaps, internalize some of these feelings – so much for the "presumption of innocence." Imagine, worse yet, jurors see the lawyer hired or appointed to represent that client sending off the same signals. The body language gives jurors great pause when assessing the client. In particular, when the client's lawyer exhibits resentful body language, jurors are given the "ok" to feel the same resentment toward the client.

It is certainly the best practice to genuinely like your client, but as trial lawyers, we do not always choose clients. Regardless, our body language must send positive signals about them to the jurors. Incidentally, the converse holds true as well, as your client's body language toward you, is also important.

HOW AND TO WHAT EXTENT CAN WE READ JURORS?

Whether lawyers, trial consultants or anyone else in the courtroom can "read" jurors to the extent that they can accurately determine which jurors are on their side is debatable. However, body language does at times provide clues about jurors' attitudes. We surmise that generally, jurors that open themselves up to us will more likely accept what we do while those who close their bodies off to us, with arms folded for instance, will not. We might further assume based on body language that people sending supportive, positive signals are on our side.

Supportive and positive signals include, among others, open gestures, nodding as we speak, and at times even a smile. Alternatively, we usually view people that send unsupportive, negative signals through their body language, such as closed gestures, or perhaps stone-faced looks, to be less favorable to our cause.

However, in speaking to people after presentations, in court or otherwise, we know these assessments are not foolproof and always reliable. Specifically, we might find out that people who were signaling negative body language to us actually took great pleasure in our presentation, while those with open body language may have had little or no use for what we said. At times, a person with outwardly negative signals, sitting with folded arms and a serious facial expression, has greatly enjoyed our presentation.

This dynamic applies, for instance, to job interviews. As an interviewee, you might feel comfortable throughout an interview, interpreting the interviewers' smiles and positive messages as a sign that the job is yours. But when the dust settles, this may not be the case. Rather, the interviewers simply did their best to be polite, as they consciously tried not to signal through their body language that your chance of getting the position is futile and will never become reality.

Whether genuine or fair, right or wrong, the white lies sometimes sent through body language are a fact of life. Alternatively, the interviewers, for some reason, may not want to give off that you are a strong candidate for the job, and thus they send little by way of positive signals through their body language.

These misdirection signals surface at times in court and we need look no further than our verdicts to know this to be the case. A juror that smiled at defense counsel in a criminal trial during the course of several days will sit just as comfortably as everyone else when a guilty verdict is read. As that juror gets polled, they readily and comfortably admit that "this was then and is now their verdict."

On the contrary, jurors who sent negative body language to defense counsel during the trial, often sitting with closed arms and a stern face, will reveal after trial that they never believed a word of the prosecution's case and they simply could not wait to sign a "not guilty" verdict form.

Other factors may also contribute to the misdirection of signals. The outwardly negative gesture of closing one's arms might simply mean the juror is perhaps cold or simply more comfortable sitting that way, as they are made to sit for several hours a day, in an uncomfortable, wooden chair. While we can and should be conscious of the body language of jurors, our "read" of their signals is anything but an exact science.

MEANINGFUL EYE CONTACT: CONNECT WITH THE SOUL, NOT THE SURFACE

The eyes are the path to the soul and a persuasive trial lawyer must develop, and indeed perfect, meaningful eye contact. As courtroom storytellers and persuaders, we learn how to travel effectively down this path to the soul by initially considering and understanding eye contact from the *jurors'* perspective. Like many other facets of courtroom communication, we best explore and understand eye contact from the jurors' perspective because only through their perspective can we truly discover *how and why,* in fact, the eyes are the path to the soul.

First, we put ourselves momentarily in an audience and think back to when we watched and listened to a presentation to decide which speakers, in terms of eye contact, we want to emulate. Of course we do not consider a speaker who makes no eye contact whatsoever, because obviously we must make eye contact to communicate effectively.

Let's start by considering two extremes. The first speaker stares you down, establishing a firm, demanding connection with your eyes, as if it is a stand-off or game of chicken. This speaker likely revels in a feeling of apparent dominance, believing they effectively communicated with you. Regardless of their intention, you feel like a bug pinned to the wall. Little do they realize that the eye contact left you uncomfortable at best, possibly feeling somewhat violated and probably unwilling the next time around, to even give them the chance to make eye contact. As the target on the other end of the stare down method of eye contact, we know it is uncomfortable and unsuccessful.

The attempt to connect with the soul of the audience only connected with the surface of the audience, albeit in a most uncomfortable way.

Moving from the stare down method to the opposite extreme, we consider the speaker who makes little or only fleeting eye contact. Their eyes quickly and at times frenetically meet and dart off one set of eyes after another. Never really looking at anyone in the audience, they are on an eye contact shopping spree, believing that each time their eyes "tap" someone else's eyes, they have scored again. This opposite extreme of eye contact, while perhaps not as discomforting as a stare down, is equally ineffective, as the speaker again never establishes meaningful eye contact.

Considering two opposite ends of the spectrum, we know that the appropriate amount of eye contact must lie somewhere in the middle. Though not an exact science, we begin to develop meaningful eye contact by telling a client's story to a jury with a goal of giving each juror, individually, segments of the story lasting approximately four consecutive seconds. We make the segments meaningful by warmly meeting the eyes of each juror. This does not suggest that the actual story is broken down into methodical segments lasting exactly four seconds because the story will flow and be told continuously, taking into account, of course, speaking pace and communicative pauses.

The eye contact, however, will consist of continuous segments as we change jurors approximately every four seconds, ideally keeping our eyes on one juror until we move them to the next juror. While maintaining eye contact with each juror during their segment, we imagine giving each juror something special, unique and reserved only for them. With the eyes tugging at the soul we create commonality and empathy.

When using this technique in conjunction with open, upward-facing palms, as discussed below when we discuss opening our body language, our attitude will be one of delivering something special, and the eye contact will be warm and meaningful. Between this giving attitude, open gestures and meaningful eye contact, we successfully reach the soul, rather than merely the surface, of the jurors.

After establishing effective eye contact timing, we consider the pattern of eye contact, or, whom to look at, when to look at them and in what order. From the standpoint of body language, the idea of lawyers walking "guard duty" will be discussed below. In terms of eye contact, walking "guard duty" in front of the jury box often results in an overly regimented and predictable eye contact pattern, with the lawyer simply moving eye contact up and down the line. Might this encourage jurors to tune out until it is their turn again? Possibly.

Thus, a random pattern is more effective. We look at each juror an appropriate number of times while letting no juror feel left out. Some lawyers try to make specific, usually important, points with jurors with whom they feel most comfortable, usually based on the lawyer's read of positive body language signals and determination, albeit unscientific, that the juror is on their side. This succeeds, however, if at all, only if the lawyer's base assumptions are correct.

Incidentally, we also consider the extent to which a lawyer should make eye contact with witnesses, particularly during cross-examination. This much debated subject produces two schools of thought, one recommending that you maintain near constant eye contact with a witness during cross-examination, and another, recommending that you focus on the jury, as they are the audience for the story you deliver on cross-examination. While there may not be a clear answer to this issue we discuss some of the considerations.

Maintaining relatively constant eye contact with a witness during cross-examination might help control the witness, to the extent control is part of the objective of cross-examination. When meeting a witness' eyes directly, that witness will often feel uncomfortable wandering off topic, as your eye contact serves, for lack of a better term, as a leash.

Further, while maintaining eye contact with the witness and keeping a constant watch on them, you can better read the witness' overall body language. In a somewhat misguided and domineering sense, many lawyers feel that staring down the witness gives them an edge, much like the speaker we discussed above, who wants the witness, through piercing eye contact, to feel like a bug pinned to the wall. Incidentally, many lawyers make the mistake, particularly while impeaching a witness, of trying to *convince the witness* of something. However, even an excellent cross examiner will seldom convince the witness of anything, and the best cross examiners always recognize they must convince and persuade the *jury*.

When considering eye contact on cross examination, a different and perhaps better school of thought notes the significant upside to focusing on the jurors during cross-examination. By doing so, we deliver the goods directly into the jury box, because after all, the jurors are the rightful and proper recipients of your story on cross-examination. Just as you deliver your opening statement and closing argument to the jury, your cross should be no different.

Moreover, with eyes locked on the witness, we cannot effectively deliver the story to the jurors or assess how jurors *receive and react* to a cross-examination. By focusing on the jurors, we deliver the cross story directly to them, consistent with the true spirit and purpose of cross-examination, which is to use the witness merely as a conduit through whom you deliver a story. Focusing on the jurors rather than the witness also lessens the temptation to bicker or quibble with the witness. The lawyer will more likely stay in the proper mode of cross-examination, that of giving a monologue.

Professional witnesses, police officers and some others, often learn to look at the jury when testifying. For most other witnesses, when their eyes have nowhere to go and no purpose, their shifting eyes will often detract from rather than bolster their credibility in the eyes of jurors.

BODY LANGUAGE IN GENERAL:
IT'S AN OPEN, NOT CLOSED CASE

In assessing the net effect of body language on persuasion, most agree that open gestures are generally preferable to closed gestures. We open gestures and body language by keeping arms at our sides with elbows slightly bent and our hands in front of our body with palms facing upward. This gesture shows your audience that you are vulnerable, trustworthy and open to information and all comers. Thus, to send effective signals to jurors, we open our gestures and body language.

A common closed gesture is to stand with arms crossed and folded in front of your body. This gesture non-verbally signals to your audience that along the lines of communication, you are closed for business and not interested in anything incoming, including information. A correlative effect of closing oneself off is the signal that we might actually be hiding something. This closing of gestures is contrary to our purpose on trial, particularly when jurors are the true aces in the courtroom, and along with our client, the people that matter most to us.

Our body language should signal to jurors that we are open to them, interested in everything about them and not hiding anything. To create trust, we non-verbally signal an open line of communication.

As discussed with eye contact, a significant message we send jurors when we speak with open hands is the concept of actually giving something to them. Interestingly, statues, both ancient and modern, often have open and vulnerable poses, many with an open hand, signaling generosity and giving.

Our open hands in court, while "holding" a part of our client's story, and in conjunction with warm and sincere eye contact, create a genuine sense of giving each juror a valuable part of the story, and symbolically reveal an open, honest line of communication.

TELLING A STORY WITH OUR HANDS

While we start with open gestures and body language, our hands can and will do much more to persuasively tell our client's story in court. We will illustrate, define, accentuate, and above all, *paint*. Our hands create images and paint pictures to supplement verbal presentations. Indeed, when we use our hands effectively, we create indelible images in the jurors' minds. Ideally, they will take those images back to the jury room. After some conscious practice through some of the exercises discussed above, lawyers will do this with an unconscious capability.

We must first, however, take a conscious look at how we sometimes use our hands ineffectively, by noting some common problems lawyers have incorporating their hands effectively into courtroom presentations. Among the gestures to eliminate, perhaps the most common is nervous energy getting channeled into the hands. The tendency to fidget with the hands, pull on fingers, play with rings or simply clasp one hand with the other, is usually an attempt to release nervous energy. These are problematic habits that must be broken.

Regardless of intention, nervous fidgeting with hands will inevitably distract jurors from the story by becoming an intermittent focus of their attention. Worse yet, fidgeting can significantly belie the speaker's confidence. After long hours of painstaking preparation, a presentation suffers needlessly when a speaker appears uncertain. This uncertainty belies the speaker's confidence and their commitment to client and cause. Rather than properly channeling energy in the right place, the telling of the client's story, the energy gets released through distracting, fidgety hands.

A different version of the same problem, which is equally unpersuasive, is the fallback gestures used when speakers want to appear in control, but have yet to comfortably use their hands openly and persuasively. These include the politician's favorite, among others, as the speaker presses their thumbs to both their index and middle finger, as if all three fingers are glued together. Other speakers use the "hammer fist," as it is called in the martial arts, where points are continuously emphasized by pounding both fists in sync, in a downward motion.

Perhaps the courtroom setting encourages bad habits and causes lawyers to fidget or use these odd gestures. Certainly, very few people use these gestures in everyday conversation and storytelling. Regardless, lawyers should recognize and relearn the easier, more effective and natural way to speak with the hands, a method they used as children and for most of their lives.

Thinking back to a young age, before exposure to an academic system that emphasized right and wrong, we told stories accompanied by unconscious hand gestures which amplified the story. For example, when we told our parents that something was *"big",* we spread our arms out as far as they would go, to *show* them what we were talking about. When we told someone about the baseball player that hit the home run, we accompanied the story by a swinging motion, as if we were swinging the bat, followed by a hand extending upward and outward toward the sky, to show the ball's trajectory into orbit. Perhaps the best example is watching a young child in a Halloween costume acting out and physically portraying their character.

As children tell stories, their hands are an integral, natural and effective part of their storytelling. As children, we used our hands to accentuate stories and paint visual pictures for our listeners, and we did so naturally and unconsciously, unaware it was one of our greatest, persuasive storytelling skills. Indeed, we used this skill with *unconscious capability*.

Somewhere along the way, however, someone dissuaded us from using this skill. Perhaps we were encouraged to tone it down, speak like a grownup, or made to feel foolish for physical portrayals. Luckily, we were only partially stripped of this skill, as we still see glimpses of this talent, not so much in the courtroom, but certainly in everyday natural conversations.

The first step of regaining and relearning the effective use of our hands for the courtroom, is to jump back in time, to a different and perhaps better day, when we openly, effectively and naturally expressed ourselves without a constant cloud of adult or academic judgment hanging over our heads.

To eliminate nerves and fidgety hands in court, simply imagine yourself speaking freely and unhindered, as if in your living room, a bar or another place of comfort, where you are not being judged. Then, incorporate all the things you do with your hands to tell stories in that comfortable environment. Once you *forget you are in a courtroom,* you will use your hands unconsciously and effectively. On a higher, more creative and persuasive level, think about everything you can do with your hands in court to tell stories.

When we used emotional range to brainstorm, prepare and practice courtroom presentations, we willingly went overboard, knowing we could always, if necessary, tone it down. Likewise, as we practice with our hands to prepare for court, we will also go over the top, again knowing that we can always tone it down.

We should practice, for instance, by not only telling our story, but also by demonstrating the entire story with our hands, using them at every moment to show what is happening. We will of course tone this down for the courtroom, but this practice is invaluable. Incidentally, skilled storytellers with speaking disabilities ably and persuasively present entire stories without saying a word.

We can go back, for instance, and tell a portion of Mr. Smith's story while using our hands as storytelling tools. Through our hands we show every part of the story. Perhaps as we prepare and practice our case we note some excessive hand gestures that are over the top for courtroom purposes. But, again, as with our exploration of emotional range, we should go over the top as we develop and explore hand gestures and body language. The willingness to experiment during trial preparation increases our awareness of body language and our ability to use our hands to paint pictures and create images to enhance our story.

From a practical standpoint, the willingness to explore and improve the use of our hands will do three things. First, we relearn and redevelop the ability to "speak" naturally with our hands while telling stories, reclaiming a skill that was severely diminished years ago. Second, we create the *habit* of using our hands effectively, rather than simply relying and falling back on the ineffective, stale gestures used by politicians and others, who, for most intents and purposes, we should not seek to emulate in court, simply because we don't know what to do with our hands. We no longer need to glue our thumb to our middle finger and forefinger, because we now use our hands in an unbridled and unlimited number of ways to tell our story. Lastly, we no longer gesture with our hands consciously. Rather, we develop the unconscious capability of using our hands naturally and effectively to supplement our story.

PENS AND POINTING

For some odd, inexplicable reason, lawyers fondly hold pens while speaking in court. Inevitably, needlessly wielding and swinging a pen distracts jurors and on some level sucks their attention away from the important content of the story. More importantly, the pen limits and impedes the hands from being used effectively. How amusing it is when a lawyer stands up to perform at trial with a pen in hand, particularly on cross-examination, as if to send a message to the witness or jurors that, "I will now seek and destroy, as I am *armed* with this deadly weapon. If you thought I was serious before, you ain't seen nothing yet! I am now packing a fully loaded ballpoint." Other lawyers stand and check things off their page as they tell a story in court, perhaps to say, "You can see I've got a pen, I'm very meticulous and will not miss any fact." Regardless, the net effect is not a good one.

Many newscasters, and in particular sportscasters, cannot separate themselves from their pen as they deliver news. On Saturday Night Live, it is likely intended and received as a joke. For real newscasters, perhaps it gives a feeling of being astute, prepared or ready for anything. In reality, the pen serves at best to distract, and at worst, to annoy the audience. Likewise, lawyers with pens distract the jurors and detract from the story presentation.

Enough about trying a case with a pen in your hand – Don't do it! If you feel the need to write something during trial, it will usually be important enough to the case that you will not forget it. However, if you absolutely need to write something down, simply pause, write, put the pen down and move on.

When used infrequently and for a good reason, a lawyer can sometimes use a pen with demonstrative appeal. When a pen is used sparingly, for instance, perhaps as a prop when something important and particularly helpful to your case occurs, jurors might recognize and become conditioned to the fact that when the pen comes out, you have just scored a major point. Perhaps when witnesses are impeached with inconsistent statements, the pen signals to the jurors, "here we go again." In all other regards, we should not try cases with a pen in our hand.

Another odd but common habit of many lawyers is to overuse the pointing gesture, a gesture usually used as a show of power and/or control. Pointing will sometimes annoy listeners and at other times be offensive, particularly when lawyers point at jurors. Whether directed at jurors, a witness or opposing counsel, pointing is usually among the least desirable gestures available, and like most courtroom communication, must be understood from the audience's point of view.

We generally associate pointing with stern, confrontational situations, often involving discipline. It usually evokes uncomfortable, bad, and often caustic, feelings. We picture an adult, especially a parent or teacher, sternly warning or reprimanding a child, either before or after the child misbehaves. Afterward, the child is ready to go hop in bed and crawl under their sheets, and the parent is ready to issue a one-way ticket to the moon. Inevitably, the communication causes uncomfortable feelings on both sides.

Pointing is also a kissing cousin of anger and frequent precursor to violence. Often, two people pointing at one another signals impending doom and physical violence. Indeed, if those people had tails, their tails would be raised stiffly in the air signaling a battle.

Pointing at jurors conjures up the negative feelings of the gesture. It is distasteful and contrary to the feelings of openness, goodwill and credibility we want to establish. Even with opposing witnesses, counsel or opposing clients, it is an unnecessary, ineffective and overly domineering way of trying to establish control or power, and will at times evoke in jurors the negative experiential feelings associated with the gesture. These feelings are inconsistent with our purpose at trial.

Will we ever point in court? Yes, perhaps at times our case theory necessitates that we point to supplement an emotion, if the pointing gesture evokes feelings appropriate to our story. Assume a client in a self-defense situation became embroiled in a heated, finger-pointing conversation with the complaining witness before turning to violence to protect himself. To get jurors to understand, on an *emotional* level, how the client felt when the complaining witness aggressively and threateningly pursued him, we might point to evoke the emotion of the story, and in particular, to demonstrate why the client was justified in defending himself. Outside of pointing to evoke emotion consistent with our story, however, we should eschew its use.

POSTURE AND MOVEMENT:
PLUG IN THE FEET, MOVE WITH A PURPOSE

With our hands telling stories effectively, we focus on movement around the courtroom. We start by acknowledging some common bad habits and unpersuasive courtroom movement and then focus on how to move effectively in court. Among two of the most common bad habits of lawyers in court are bad posture and, more frequently, using unnecessary and inefficient movement, usually consisting of aimless meandering or wandering around the courtroom.

Bad posture does not exude capability, confidence or credibility. Slouching or slumping over exudes an attitude that is at best carefree, lazy and disinterested, and at worst, the too cool for school attitude of "I don't give a crap about anything."

Lawyers need to be particularly cautious about the temptation to use and lean on lecterns, or to use lecterns at all. We discuss this more later. With a hand on either side of a lectern, notwithstanding the other problems associated with lecterns, there is a significant temptation to slouch over, particularly when the speaker is taller than the lectern. Slouching, slumping or leaning on a lectern sends the wrong message to jurors.

To improve posture, we start with a basic stance, often used as a starting point for athletic stances, that exudes confidence and from which all other courtroom movement evolves. The stance is as follows: stand up straight and tall, with feet about shoulder width apart and arms at your side. We stand straight, feel natural and look confidant. From this stance all courtroom movement will flow, with hands ready to help us tell our story.

Unfortunately, due to nerves or simply because some lawyers have not given thought to movement, they habitually move unnecessarily, inefficiently and distractingly in court. They wander aimlessly while speaking and, perhaps unconsciously, meander about the courtroom, without regard to their story and the effect of their movement on jurors. Sometimes, this habit becomes one of serving guard duty, as the lawyer marches systematically and rigidly up and down the jury box in a regular and constant pattern.

Similar to holding a pen while speaking, aimless and unnecessary wandering distracts jurors. Constant movement inevitably, albeit at a barely conscious level, detracts from jurors' ability to focus on your story. Their heads will move back and forth like a tennis audience when a lawyer never stands still. On the opposite end of this spectrum is the somewhat lifeless presentation of a lawyer who rarely moves at all, standing still for unusually long periods of time. This absence of movement can lull jurors to sleep due to the stagnation.

How then, do we move effectively in the courtroom to best guarantee the jurors' undivided attention on our story? We should follow two basic rules, although certainly not without exception. One, we should generally plug our feet into the ground when speaking, and second, we should move with a purpose.

Imagine, for a moment, standing still in the basic stance discussed above with your feet actually "plugged" into the ground, as if in an electrical socket. Imagine further that the power derived from the socket is necessary to start speaking. If and when you pull either foot from the socket you pull out the plug and lose that power.

By plugging your feet into the ground before speaking, we habitually stand firm and strong every time we speak. Firm and strong does not equate to stiff, rigid, perfectly still or robotic. Rather, we stand confidently while staying relaxed and fluid, without extraneous movement. This habit of plugging in your feet eliminates needless wandering and nervous energy, particularly in your legs. You can forget about your legs and concentrate on presenting a story.

Certainly we do not limit ourselves to one "outlet" on the floor as of course, there are several outlets. Where exactly are the outlets, so you know where you can "plug in" to speak? The short answer is you can place outlets anywhere you desire on the courtroom floor and we later discuss in more depth the strategic placement of outlets in relation to courtroom physicality and your story.

For now, we discuss courtroom movement in terms of *when* and *why* we move. The when and why of courtroom movement is based on always moving *with a purpose,* rather than simply wandering or being driven to move by nerves. The greater sense of what we are doing guides effective courtroom movement. Whether you pick spots on the floor in advance or select them as you go, movement from one spot to another will usually be dictated by a natural, purposeful break in your story.

For instance, a natural break in your story, often times a transition in the story used effectively with a communicative pause, provides an ideal time to move from one plug to another. Incidentally, as you move, you will obviously break briefly from the eye contact pattern discussed above until you get to another "plug." This movement is productive, however, as you can collect your thoughts and give the jurors valuable time to digest and reflect upon your story.

THE COURTROOM

Considering its space and other props, the courtroom provides several things we can use physically to make our story effective. Though courtroom layouts differ, in some respects most, out of necessity, have consistent features. Most courtrooms have the following features: a witness stand, two counsel tables, the judge's bench and a jury box. Most, if not all, given the public nature of trials, also have a viewing area for spectators. Most importantly, a courtroom has a "well," of sorts, accessible to the rest of the courtroom and generally in front of the judge's bench and jury box.

COMMITTING TO INVISIBLE SPACE

Through the freeze tag exercise we developed spontaneity and body language while simultaneously exploring our ability to recognize and use invisible space. We will use the invisible courtroom space, usually in the "well" of the courtroom in front of the jury box, to persuade.

Long before my introduction to improv, I learned and used this concept by happenstance. I had actually used it several times before consciously understanding or recognizing the full dynamic and significance of what was happening. Later, I learned that improv would enhance this concept and make this tool more effective.

One cannot overstate the importance of studying crime scenes and other physical scenes that are significant to telling a story in court. Visiting scenes allows a lawyer to develop clear visuals, bring images into the courtroom and present the scenes in the invisible courtroom space. During opening statements, closing arguments, and particularly on direct and cross-examination, we can create realities using invisible courtroom space to explain a story to jurors.

For instance, during opening statement (and later closing argument), we create a "scene," as if it exists in the invisible space of the courtroom. We pretend and acknowledge the scene does exist and at all times we respect the space. During both direct and cross-examination, we might actually walk witnesses through the pretend scene created in the invisible space.

Without consciously understanding what was happening, I used this technique as a new lawyer and recognized that invisible scenes served as a great aid to tell stories in court. Sometimes, perhaps, the created space was simply a crutch that helped me visualize a scene. Regardless, the scenes certainly helped create a physical, albeit pretend, reality for jurors. By maintaining and respecting that reality consistently throughout an entire trial, I used the invisible space scenes to guide jurors through the story. Additionally, for my own peace of mind, I could safely and easily refer back to specific scenes, always aware of where each scene was located in the courtroom. With repetition and consistency, jurors also started to "see" the same scenes.

Significantly, opposing counsels, at different points during the trial, would most often acknowledge and use my scenes and my space in exactly the same place in the courtroom. When opponents use the space *you* create, undoubtedly, your story gains plausibility because opponents begin to try their case on your stage. Unable to resist the tempting invitation to jump into your stage and your space, they inevitably support your reality, story and theory.

When an improv skit creates a bartender and bar, no one walks "through" the bar. Likewise, in court, once an invisible scene is created in court, the space should be respected, in a sense that the lawyer not "walk through" that space.

For instance, we created an invisible scene in a trial to demonstrate the implausibility of a complaining witness' ("cw") version of a fight. The cw alleged that the accused kicked him in the middle of the back as the cw stood three feet off the ground on a step that led to the cab of a large semi-truck. Using the invisible scene of the truck's steps directly in front of the jury box, we demonstrated the impossibility of the accused kicking that high in the air. Though facts tend to speak for themselves, the scene helped emphasize the impossibility of the cw's story.

Setting the scene on cross-examination, the cw acknowledged and committed to the height of the step he stood on when kicked. Interestingly, and as is often the case when a scene is created out of invisible space, opposing counsel more than once referenced and acknowledged the same scene in exactly the same invisible space in the courtroom. The scene aided in telling the story and helping the jury envision the scene. Perhaps more importantly, opposing counsel validated the scene and implicitly lent credence to our story by bringing the jurors' attention to the invisible space.

Even without any physical "props" in court, we can create a tangible, palpable reality in court by committing to scenes in invisible space, similar to an improv skit.

MOVEMENT ACCORDING TO STORYLINE, SPACE AND JUXTAPOSITION

In addition to using invisible space, our story can guide and give purpose to our courtroom movement in other ways to prevent willy-nilly movement throughout the courtroom.

For instance, we can juxtapose two ideas or two sides of the story. Let's take for example a self-defense case where you want to demonstrate the aggressive nature of the complaining witness ("cw"). Your story will portray the cw as an angry and threatening aggressor, verbally and physically. The cw was at all times the hunter as he loudly intimidated the accused. The accused minded his own business and went about his day until being involuntarily thrust into a bad situation where the cw physically attacked him, leaving him no choice but to defend himself. To juxtapose cw and accused, we use movement and courtroom space.

By dictionary definition, juxtaposition involves putting two things side by side. In the courtroom, we can do so with contrasting effect by selecting two spots in the courtroom, one for each of the two people (or ideas) we want to juxtapose. Using two spots in the jury's view, we commit our two ideas, in this case actual people from the case, to one of the two spots.

We assign one spot, "A," to the cw, and another spot, "B," to the accused. Just as we remained respectful and consistent using our invisible space to create scenes, we will likewise remain consistent with these two spots. As we tell our story and plug our feet into spot "A," we create everything the cw represents. By portraying his anger and perhaps even telling the story from the cw's point of view, we paint his aggression. By consistently associating spot "A" with the cw, the jurors will associate spot "A" with everything he represented.

When we plug our feet into spot "B," however, we will juxtapose the accused with cw, by delivering our story in terms of emotion, content and perhaps point of view, in a way that accurately represents the accused and his predicament. Through our commitment to and portrayal of the accused on spot "B," the jurors will associate that spot with him.

As storytellers assisted by courtroom space, our story informs and guides our movement. We move purposefully and deliberately rather than randomly and willy-nilly, as we create a clearly defined and memorable distinction between cw and the accused. This is one example. With our story as our guide, there are many other creative ways we can use the courtroom space to enhance our story.

NO "DIRECT" VIEW OF THE LAWYER DURING DIRECT EXAMINATION

A lawyer conducts much, if not most, of a trial from the "well" of the courtroom, within full view of the jurors. During voir dire, opening statement, closing argument, and cross-examination, the lawyer is the focal point and main attraction, and as such, is featured in the show. Direct examination, however, differs somewhat, as the witness becomes the focus and main attraction.

An effective and well-conducted direct examination requires a tremendous amount of work and preparation on the part of the lawyer. However, at trial, the main focus is on the witness and the witness immediately and notably enters the credibility fray. As such, the witness must fend for themselves while the lawyer exits the stage and gets out of the way.

We certainly advise witnesses to speak directly to jurors and some witnesses have no difficulty doing so. Professional witnesses such as law enforcement officials train themselves to speak to jurors when testifying. But the average lay witness probably feels more comfortable speaking directly to the lawyer during direct examination because the two parties developed a comfort level during their extensive case preparation.

However, like a professional witness, a lay witness should likewise direct their story to the jury, and the lawyer's positioning can encourage and facilitate this. Rather than standing in the "well" of the courtroom, within direct view of jurors, the lawyer on direct examination should move aside, so as to encourage and allow the witness to take center stage and speak directly to the jury.

Depending on the courtroom layout, a lawyer accomplishes this by standing behind the jury box in an effort to keep the jury box between themselves and the witness. This encourages the witness to speak to the jurors. Even when directing a witness who is comfortable speaking to the jury, it is best for the lawyer to move off the stage so the lawyer's physical presence does not detract from the witness' presentation. We can bolster this by asking the witness to "tell," "explain" or "show" something in particular to the jurors.

LIMITS ON PERSUASIVE MOVEMENT: LECTERNS AND THE NEED TO REMAIN SEATED

We strive to have an unbridled use of physicality in the courtroom in our pursuit to persuade. Some jurisdictions, however, restrict lawyers by requiring that lawyers stand behind a lectern. Other jurisdictions require that the lawyer remain within arm's length of the lectern, while yet others require counsel to remain seated during parts of their trial presentation.

Sometimes jocularly referred to as the "wooden dress," a lectern is a platform that typically serves as a holder for the notes of a public speaker. Unfortunately, a lectern literally and figuratively creates a barrier between a lawyer and the jury. It is designed for presenters rather than persuaders.

Lecterns are commonly used in houses of worship, and thus, we first consider a lectern in that context, noting how well-spoken, and indeed, persuasive religious leaders use them. They commonly use lecterns during ceremonies to deliver religious readings. However, when it comes to persuasively imploring the congregation to give money, that same preacher typically eliminates the barrier and seldom stands behind the lectern. Rather, the preacher mingles in the audience, literally and figuratively opening up to the congregation by eliminating the separation between speaker and congregation. Notably and symbolically, lectern manufacturers now make glass lecterns to minimize the separation between speakers and congregations. The glass lectern breaks down the barrier and creates a greater feeling of closeness between the two.

In a courtroom, a lectern literally stands between a lawyer and the jury, cutting off jurors from the lawyer's persuasive body language, among other things. Worse yet, as discussed above, the lectern tempts the lawyer to "ride" it as a safety net by firmly gripping it on both sides, limiting the ability to persuade with hands and other body language.

Figuratively, lecterns implement a barrier between the lawyer and jury by creating a disparity in status between the lawyer and jurors. Some houses of worship intentionally create a disparity in status, given the higher status of religious leaders. The same holds true, perhaps, in a teacher-student relationship. The lectern symbolizes that the person behind it must be respected and, in some situations revered, in as much as they are up on a pedestal, of sorts.

We do not want this dynamic in court. In fact, we want to create the opposite effect. A lectern serves well as a place to set down notes, but we should not glue or anchor ourselves to it as a center piece. Our body language and communication is more persuasive when the jury can see us, and we are open to them, both literally and figuratively.

Some local courtroom rules exacerbate the inherent problems of lecterns by dictating that lawyers must either stand behind or within an arm's length of the lectern at all times. This rule is certainly a "goose and gander" situation, as it equally limits both sides. However, a persuader must do everything possible to escape the lectern's shackles, which usually means doing everything possible to move away from the lectern. To escape from behind the lectern and break down that barrier, we must find any and every excuse, including approaching counsel table or the witness stand, perhaps to show witnesses exhibits.

Some jurisdictions restrict lawyers by requiring that they remain seated while presenting important parts of their case. Like the lectern rule, this limits lawyers, creates an unnecessary barrier between the lawyer and jurors and distinctly disadvantages lawyers who would otherwise persuade with effective body language. This seating requirement certainly places a premium on effectively using hands to tell a story because the hands might be the only body part visible to the jury. In addition to using the hands to accentuate the story, the lawyer should creatively break free from the counsel table often, perhaps to use physical exhibits.

HOW WE "EXHIBIT" OURSELVES IN COURT

We will often handle physical objects in court. Some are used only for demonstrative purposes, others are introduced into evidence and yet others go back to the jury room for deliberations. Because we constantly send physical signals to jurors, the way we handle exhibits certainly sends a message to jurors. Specifically, our handling of exhibits sends a clear message to the jurors as to how *they* should feel about the exhibit.

For instance, while defending a drug prosecution, we impeach a police officer with an inconsistent statement from an official police report. We will later handle the prosecution's main evidence - an inventoried bag of heroin. While impeaching the officer, assume we want the jury to believe and rely on the statement in the report. The report is of biblical proportion and we hold it as such. We hold the report as if holding something sacred or perhaps as we would hold valuable glassware. Our body language clearly signals to the jurors the significance of the report and we want them to "feel" its importance.

Our handling of the bag of heroin sends a different message. We hold it perhaps like we would hold a dead mouse by the tail. We signal our disdain for the bag and invite the jurors to feel our disassociation with the drugs. Like using tone of voice to create and enhance verbal messages, here we use body language to do the same.

X.

IMPROV'S LAST LESSON: SMILE

"Sometimes your joy is the source of your smile, but sometimes your smile can be the source of your joy."

— Thich Nhat Hanh

Improv has a great way of producing genuine smiles and laughs. Though smiling and laughter is simply a byproduct of improv, it is important nonetheless as both are undoubtedly healthy.

Smiling, in particular, also has a place in the courtroom. When we smile, we gain credibility in the eyes of those around us. People like us when we smile. This should not be lost on us in court, and within reason, smiling serves us well.

XI.

ADDITIONAL FOOD FOR THOUGHT

"The difference between ordinary and extraordinary is practice."

— Vladimir Horowitz

"A wrong note played timidly is a wrong note. A wrong note played with authority is an interpretation."

— The Violin Channel

"To play a wrong note is insignificant, to play without passion is unforgivable."

— Beethoven

"The difficulty lies not so much in developing new ideas as in escaping from old ones."

— John Maynard Keynes

"True storytelling reveals meaning without committing the error of defining it."

— Hannah Arendt

"I really have no interest in likability when it comes to characters. It's always about credibility, and to be credible you have to seem human."

— Gilliam Flynn

"Never, never try to be funny! The actors must be serious. Only the situation must be absurd. Funny is in the writing, not in the performing. If the situation isn't absurd, no amount of joke will help."

— Mel Brooks

"Sometimes you have to play a long time
to be able to play like yourself."

— Miles Davis

"I think you have to have a theme. At least I do.
I think you need something to always go back to."

— Eric Roth

"I thought drama was when actors cried.
But drama is when the audience cries."

— Frank Capra

"Your subplot should increase the emotion
of the main story and/or add deeper meaning
that comes from the theme of the story."

— Screenwritingu.com

"Have no fear of perfection – you'll never achieve it."

— Salvador Dali

"There is only one plot.
Things are not what they seem."

— Jim Thompson

ABOUT THE AUTHOR

Terence MacCarthy has taught Trial Advocacy extensively around the country and trained experienced lawyers as well as law students. Through his lectures and small group teaching infused with Improv, he has earned a reputation as an excellent and effective teacher and trainer in the areas of Trial Advocacy, storytelling and communication.

He has served as a faculty member for many distinguished Trial Advocacy programs, including the National Criminal Defense College, the Administrative Office of the United States Courts and the University of Chicago Law School's Mandel Legal Aid Clinic. He is an Adjunct Professor of Law at the DePaul University College of Law where he teaches Advanced Trial Advocacy.

MacCarthy served for twenty years with the Cook County Public Defender's Office, working as an Assistant Public Defender, and for his last seven years, as an Attorney Supervisor in the Felony Trial Division at the George N. Leighton Criminal Court Building at "26th and California." He tried more than 500 cases including complex felonies and capital murder. While trying bench and jury trials he earned a reputation as an excellent trial lawyer and advocate. He was elected Judge of the Circuit Court of Cook County in 2010.

MacCarthy graduated from The University of Illinois at Champaign Urbana and the DePaul University College of Law. For questions about training, please email: glissandostrings@yahoo.com.

BODY LANGUAGE: THE UNIVERSAL LANGUAGE

Persuasive courtroom body language bolsters our client's story. At times we use body language to make a specific record of distance or some other physical demonstration. Otherwise, body language is most often not evidence in a case. Thus, while body language is often not discussed as demonstrative evidence, it is undoubtedly and undeniably intertwined with, and integral to, courtroom presentations.

From the standpoint of status, we recognize the constant signals we send to and read from other people. The body language of peers, for instance, might be relaxed, comfortable and disarmed as they sit with equals waiting for a meeting to start. However, when the company CEO walks in, that body language likely changes to attentive, upright, deferential and respectful. Our body language constantly changes, based on the status of those around us.

In court, body language is constant and pervasive and we likewise send and read signals. Often in the absence of a verbal exchange, our body language continues to send signals and we continue to read the body language of others. During voir dire and the remainder of the trial, we remain attentive to the jurors' reactions to our case and our client.

While body language is perhaps more apparent and noticeable while speaking, "to-from" messages also continue during periods of silence. From the moment we walk into the courtroom, our body language sends signals to those around us and we need to be conscious of the messages we send, so those messages best benefit our client.